THE SUNDAY TIMES

Using the Internet Smarter and Faster

GW00722395

Brooke Broadbent

⬡ KOGAN PAGE | *CREATING SUCCESS*

First published in the United States in 1998 by Crisp Publications, Inc.
1200 Hamilton Court, Menlo Park, California 94025-9600, USA

First published in Great Britain in 2000
by Kogan Page Limited
120 Pentonville Road
London N1 9JN

The views expressed in this book are those of the author and are not necessarily the same as those of Times Newspapers Ltd.

British Library Cataloguing in Publication Data

A CIP record for this book is available from the British Library.

ISBN 0 7494 3324 8

Typeset by Jean Cussons Typesetting, Diss, Norfolk
Printed and bound in Great Britain by Clays Ltd, St Ives plc

contents

acknowledgements   vii
how to use this book   viii
introduction   1

1. debunking Net myths   3

2. cracking open the Net's treasure chest   5
   increase your net profit and get results with the Net 6

3. keeping track of your key Net information   8
   revving up the speed of your modem 8; speeding up
   your modem 10

4. six attributes of skilled Net users   11
   1. know your operating system 11; 2. see more details
   on the screen 12; 3. get comfortable 12; 4. use precise
   computer terminology 12; 5. remain cool 13; 6. be
   confident to 'try things' 13

5. Windows Explorer and Windows   14
   open your mind to Windows 15; Windows 98 17

6. obtaining and using the latest versions of Net software   19
   an aversion to new versions? 20

7. tooling your searches   22
    behind the scenes of search tools 23

8. mission accomplished with a search   26

9. making sense out of Net error messages   28

10. saving your Net treasures   30

11. keyboard shortcuts   32

12. Help is on the way   34
    how to access Help resources in Windows 34;
    Help: seeing is believing, doing is understanding 36

13. exploring Help and pull-down menus   38
    steps in exploring Help and pull-down menus 39

14. freeing space on your hard drive   41

15. using the Net proactively   43

16. chat, newsgroups, e-mail and mailing lists   45

17. the chatter about chat   47

18. the scoop on newsgroups   49

19. mastering e-mail   51
    which e-mail software will it be? 51; saving time and
    money with e-mail attachments 52; don't leave home
    without e-mail access 53; mastering business rules
    for e-mail 56

20. getting advice from mailing lists   58

21. netiquette for newgroups and mailing lists   60

22. intranets for business   62
    grasping intranet basics 62; put people in touch using
    an intranet 64; intranets are cost effective 65

23. browsing information about intranets and the
    Internet   66

24. netting software for your intranet site   70

25. exploring features in Internet Explorer 5   72
    featuring Internet Explorer 73

26. using the World Wide Web productively   75
    to Web site or not to Web site 75

27. producing Web documents   78
    preparing Web documents using Microsoft Word 78

28. weaving results into your Web site   81

29. spinning online presentations for the Web   83
    creating hyperlinks in your Web page 84; practice
    makes good Web sites 85

30. plan your work and work your plan   86
    my plan to drive more safely on the Web 87

31. managing your surfing time and costs   88

32. zapping viruses   90
    virus alert! 91

33. the keys to Internet security   93
    feeling secure in Internet Explorer and Netscape 95

34. canning spam   97

35. accepting cookies from strangers   99

36. looking ahead   **101**
personal action plan to learn more about the Net 101;
paying attention to Bill the gatekeeper 102; Web sites
103; associations 103; business news 104; training
and education 104; 21st-century 'cyberspeak' 107

glossary of terms   **109**

acknowledgements

Many people play crucial roles in producing a book. I appreciate the advice, encouragement, and professional services of the fine folks at Crisp Publications. I would like to express my gratitude to people who reviewed this book, gave it a 'field test,' and offered insightful feedback. Many thanks to Patricia Broadbent, Joanna Hauser, Iman Faris, Lise Froidevaux, Leo Gabourie, Lorrie Gabourie, Mary King, Bill Loucks, Bill Myer, Beth Nickle, Allan Shipley, and Jocelyn Shipley.

how to use this book

The focus of *Using the Internet* is learning and fun. You will learn the meaning of Internet lingo, how to use key software features and other useful tips to use the Internet smarter and faster. You will be able to use the skills we teach to deepen your knowledge of other Internet topics you choose to learn in the future. If you get a charge out of succeeding, then the easy-to-follow instructions will put a smile on your face.

Approach this book as strategically as you would a buffet meal. Picture an array of platters spread before you. Choose in the quantity and order you prefer, and can digest. You might take a timid taste here, or a heaped helping there. There are tips on getting started, core Internet skills, communicating with the Internet, intranets and business, the World Wide Web and Web pages, avoiding the pitfalls of the Internet, looking ahead and a glossary of terms. Using your browser productively is critical, so several explanations are offered. *Bon appetit!*

Using the Internet can help you decide what to do about a host of Net issues, including whether you should give out your credit card information over the Net, accepting 'cookies', making your computer secure, what your organization can do with an intranet, and whether you should move up to new software. It will help you learn about Internet search tools, how to manage e-mail, and the treasures you find on the Web.

This is a self-study book. Read it with a pencil in your hand to underline and make notes in the margin. Although the Net will change, this book will serve as an ongoing reference. It is also a job aid. Turn on your computer. Go about your work. When you run into an Internet snag, check in this book and you will find practical advice to help you resolve your Net dilemmas.

A few words about conventions used in this guide: **Bold** text indicates words you will find on your screen, normally in software menus. An example of this is **Help** from the toolbar in Microsoft Internet Explorer. The underlining of the 'H' indicates that you can select this item by holding down the 'Alt' key and at the same time depressing the 'H' key. Italic means a Web address or URL: *http://www.home.netscape.com/*

learning computer software

In learning software, try using the 'se ur' method (pronounced 'see er').

Letter	Stands for	Means
S	Show	Instructor or coach shows or demonstrates the software. Learners watch. This step emphasizes visual learning and gaining a conceptual overview.
E	Explain	Instructor or coach explains the software. Learners watch, listen and question. This step emphasizes visual learning, auditory learning and understanding or cognitive learning.
U	Use	Learners use the software. This step emphasizes learning that is visual and auditory, as well as tactile and kinesthetic.
R	Review	Learners review what they have done – receiving feedback from the instructor, from other learners, from the software or from other sources, including themselves. This step moves to high-level conceptual learning and while receiving feedback it involves the emotions – thus creating a memorable experience.

introduction

By using the Internet, or Net, you can send mail quickly and cheaply to people with e-mail addresses. Instead of sending illegible faxes you can send easy-to-decipher e-mail messages. By using the World Wide Web, the world is your library. Internet search tools are your catalogue. You can get worldwide news as it breaks on the Net. You can seek advice for work-related issues on Internet mailing lists and newsgroups.

Words like Internet and intranet appear everywhere these days. But what do they mean? It will help to have clear definitions as you wind your way through this book, so let's look at the meaning of a few key words.

what is the Internet?
The Internet is a massive worldwide network of interconnected computers, loosely governed internationally. The word 'Internet' means a 'network of networks' or thousands of smaller networks scattered throughout the globe. 'Internet' is also used to mean the services offered. These include the classic services of e-mail, newsgroups, and chat, as well as the more recent browsing service provided by the World Wide Web.

'Net' is normally a short form for Internet. Given their similarity, in this book, 'Net' refers to both the Internet and intranets.

what is the World Wide Web?

The World Wide Web, or Web, is a way to organize large quantities of information. The Web links computers on the Internet through hyperlinks. By clicking on a hyperlink, you can advance to another location on the Web. Commonly, hyperlinks appear on your screen as coloured, underlined text. Hyperlinks, and the World Wide Web, are made possible through HTML tags, a simple coding procedure.

what are intranets?

Think of intranets as baby Internets. Most are established by employers to provide information to employees. Intranets use the same or similar technology and software as the Internet. While most of the information on the Internet is available to everyone, intranets are more private and used for internal purposes within an organization.

what is E-mail?

E-mail, short for Electronic Mail, consists of messages sent through the Net to other people with e-mail addresses. It can be used for personal or business mail and advertising. It is fast, cheap, and hugely popular. Some people claim that in the United States more messages are sent via the Net than through the post.

debunking Net myths

The Internet and intranets are often misunderstood. Detractors say you must be a computer whiz to use the Internet, it is very costly to use, and finding information is like looking for a needle in a haystack. There is some truth in each of these statements. The Net is complex. It is changing every day. As with anything, there are costs associated with using it.

Now for the good news. If you are patient and careful about what you do, the Net will provide you with pertinent information, and at very little cost. Use the strategies listed below to deal with Internet myths.

you must be a computer whiz to use the Internet

First thing, don't worry. Anyone can learn to use the Net effectively. In fact, many people who use the Net, do not know how to use a computer for anything else. Secondly, remember that you can learn almost anything if you take it in small steps.

they have made the Net hard to understand in order to confuse ordinary people

Decide what is the best way for you to learn about the Net.

Build a support system. Learn the lingo. Identify the gaps between what you need to know and what you know now. Fill in the gaps. Learn the basics first. Try stuff. Be patient with yourself.

One of the keys to learning about the Net is to use your favourite learning style. For example, if you enjoy facts, logic, and analysis, you could read articles in computer magazines, read books or create a structured plan of action. If you prefer self-discovery, constructing concepts, or you value initiative, you could use **Help**, experiment with the menus in your software, and generally engage in hands-on activities. If you like to test theories or value structure and processes, try planning your learning, keeping track of what you learn. Or if you enjoy sharing ideas, value intuitive thinking and enjoy working towards harmony, try talking to people about the Net, and also try hands-on activities.

it is very costly to use the Net

There are ways to trim your costs when you use the Net. You can learn to use search tools effectively. Download files at off-peak times. Internet files generally download to your computer faster in the morning.

it is impossible to find stuff on the Net

Use the search tools available on the Net. They are free.

the Net is changing every day and I will never be able to keep up-to-date

If you learn the basics, you will have the building blocks needed to keep up-to-date as the Net evolves.

The information in the rest of this book will help you learn what is necessary to debunk or demystify Net myths.

cracking open the Net's treasure chest

The Net is a treasure chest of information about any subject you can name. Here are a few situations that people have faced and how they found what they needed on the Net.

Pat was preparing for a job interview and realized she knew very little about the company. She searched for the name of the potential employer, found their Web site, learned the nature of their business, impressed them with her knowledge at the interview, and got the job.

Mary had a rare disease and her doctors knew very little about it. Using a search tool, a friend of Mary's located medical information. Web sites, and e-mail addresses of support groups. Learning from others with the disease helped Mary cope.

Richard needed a copy of software that would allow him to access compressed files that his teacher had sent him attached to an e-mail file. He searched for information about compressed files using an Internet search tool. He found the software WinZip and used it to 'unzip' his files.

Allan was planning a holiday. With an Internet search tool, he located a cottage in the area where he wanted to stay. The Web site included images of interior and exterior views. Allan made all rental arrangements over the Net.

Liz was going to see a French film. Her French was rusty so she needed a little help with vocabulary. Et voilà! Searching the title of the film with a search tool, Liz found plenty of information. Reading about the film, in French, helped her enjoy the experience.

Martin was interested in buying a certain kind of car. He used a search tool to find information in a newsgroup about the kind of car he wanted to buy. He found postings from several discontented owners. He searched another make of car and found better reports – eventually buying the car.

John started an ambitious family genealogical study after his retirement. Searching on family names with a search tool, John located distant relatives. One of these had just completed extensive family genealogical research, which he shared with John.

Anne had written a project in Spanish and she wanted to check the spelling. Using a search tool, she found a Spanish spell-checking program on the Net. She checked her text, found a few errors, corrected them, then submitted her assignment and got an A.

increase your net profit and get results with the Net

Net skills can help you perform your work smarter, faster, and better. There is tangible evidence that employees are mining the wealth of the Net to the benefit of their employers. Here are a few examples of using the Net for business.

A government agency was considering the purchase of new software to replace an application they were currently using. An employee found the Web site of a vendor selling the new software, downloaded a 30-day trial copy, and tested it. The agency decided to stay with the existing package, as it seemed superior.

A consulting firm was developing software and wondered what the competition was doing. They located the competition's site, downloaded information about their software, and made comparisons.

A software salesperson received a call from a potential client. It sounded like a promising prospect but the salesperson knew precious little about the client. While talking to the client, the salesperson used a search tool to locate the client's Web site. She learned information about the client's company and immediately used it in the conversation. She made the sale.

A financial institution wanted to expand into other parts of the country. They set up a Web site and registered it with search tools. New clients from other parts of the country learned about the services offered through the Web site – resulting in new clients in other parts of the country.

Bob was looking for ways to expand his business. He decided to attract clients by publishing articles in his field of expertise. Bob used a search tool to locate an Internet mailing list dealing with the subject he wanted to write about. He subscribed. An editor placed a request for articles on the list. Bob submitted a proposal and published several articles. All arrangements, except for the formal contract, were made through e-mail.

While talking with a client on the telephone, a sales representative identified a need for detailed information to explain a complex matter to her client. While talking on the telephone, the sales rep directed the potential client to the Web site with the required information. The client and sales rep worked through the information together. The client understood the complex points, leading eventually to a sale.

keeping track of your key Net information

When setting up your e-mail, newsgroups and browser you may have to give information about your Internet Service Provider (ISP). It helps to record this information for later reference. To do this you can make notes in the chart on page 9. This information is critical if you are a home user of the Net, since you will probably be providing your own technical support with the help of your service provider. Your ISP provides this information, except for the data about your modem. Check your invoice for this information or, if your modem is installed and working, you can obtain these details by checking the modem setting in the Windows® **Control Panel**.

revving up the speed of your modem

When you are connected to the Internet, you can check out the bit rate of your connection. Simply right-click on the icon that indicates you are connected. This is the server–client image with the green light, which I find on the extreme right of my Windows task bar. I just checked and my modem is running at 26,400 bits per second (bps). Earlier in the day it was running at 28,800 bps – the maximum connection speed I can achieve through my telephone company and service provider, although my modem is rated at 33.6 kbps or 33,000 bps.

Information	Why you need it	Example	Your information
Your e-mail address	Include in outgoing e-mail so people will know where to reply	you@isp.com	
Internet Service Provider (ISP) name	Forms part of your Internet address	isp.com	
Dial-in telephone number	Connects to your ISP's computer	788 7933	
ISP mail (SMTP) server name	Go through this server to send and receive e-mail	mail.isp.com	
ISP Usenet news server name	Connects to newsgroups	news@isp.com	
ISP primary DNS	These digits are required for configuring some Net set-ups	204.191.135.2	
ISP customer support	For receiving help getting online, configuring new Net software, and technical help when you experience difficulties	0845 555 2222	
modem	Needed to configure your Net hook-up	Sportster voice 56K FAX internal	

speeding up your modem

Here are a few steps you can take to gain the maximum speed from your modem.

1. *Connect your telephone directly from the wall to the modem. Eliminate answering machines, phone line splitters, etc.*
   You need a crystal clear connection to attain your maximum connection speed. A clean telephone signal will give you a fast connection.
2. *Eliminate radio interference and static.*
   This affects the overall quality of your telephone line transmission. A clean telephone signal is needed for a maximum connection.
3. *Use a high-quality modem.*
   Generally, you get what you pay for. Higher-quality modems have more ability to work at full speed when there is noise on your line.
4. *Check with your ISP.*
   Support staff at ISP facilities often hear from clients who have problems with their modems. ISP staff can often provide information relevant for your local situation.

six attributes of skilled Net users

Have you ever noticed the behaviour of skillful Net users? They know their operating system inside-out. They see more details on the screen than less fortunate users who have problems using computers. The computer whiz sits comfortably in his or her chair, fingers gliding over the keys. When they talk about the Net, they use precise, correct vocabulary. Skilled computer users keep their cool when their systems crash. And when they are faced with a computer problem, they have the confidence required to 'try things.'

When you possess these attributes, combined with the basic knowledge of this book, you will be able to go anywhere on the Net. You will be able to do anything you want to do in cyberspace. Well, almost anything.

1. know your operating system

Start with first things first. Learn how everything functions on the Windows desktop: the My Computer icon, the Network Neighborhood icon, the Recycle Bin, the Taskbar, the Start

Button, the Start Bar, and shortcuts. Learn how to work with Windows (resizing, minimize, restore, and close buttons). If your computer came with a beginner's CD ROM or other learning material you should review it. Check out **Help** on the start bar. It explains the items listed above along with many others that will help make you comfortable using the Web.

2. see more details on the screen

Take a good long look at your browser and e-mail software. Study the menus and become familiar with all aspects of what you see on your screen. Next time you are using Internet Explorer, Netscape, Pegasus Mail, Eudora, etc., take your time and absorb everything on the screen – top, bottom, left, right.

3. get comfortable

Give yourself plenty of space. Get a comfortable set-up. Add an under-the-desk keyboard drawer if you need one. Buy an ergonomically sound chair. Slow down. Concentrate. Enjoy.

4. use precise computer terminology

Learn the right terms and use them. One reason to say you 'compose' e-mail rather than write it is that the **Help** files normally, but not always, store their information under the terms that appear in the menus. Therefore, you need to learn and use words like compose, send, retrieve, and other terms featured in your menus and help files.

remain cool

Computers and their software are becoming more complex. Glitches are prevalent, caused by programming errors, software designer oversights, and operator error. Accept that you will experience problems when you use a computer. Relax. When you have a problem, stop. Take a break. Reflect on what happened. Seek advice. Learn from glitches. The true computer whiz benefits from problems: they provide opportunities to learn.

be confident to 'try things'

If you acquire the first five attributes, this sixth one will come automatically – you will become confident in your ability and you will 'try things.'

Windows Explorer and Windows

Where did my file go? How can I be certain that I am accessing the latest version of a file? Where can I store valuable information? Windows Explorer® helps answer these questions and others.

what is Windows Explorer?

Windows Explorer maps your computer, showing what is on all hard drives, and other pertinent information. For example, you can sort your files by name, size, type and date you last modified them. This can help you to be certain that you are working with the most recent version of a file. As well, you can double-click on a file and it will start, or execute, from Windows Explorer.

why use it?

You can use Windows Explorer to see all the folders and files on your computer. That way you can manage all your information.

how do I access it?

Right click on the **Start** menu and select **Explore**.

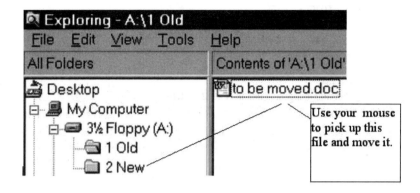

Figure 5.1. *Folders on a computer as viewed in Windows Explorer*

open your mind to Windows

Thirteen people reviewed the manuscript of this book. Much to my surprise, I learned that three of the reviewers had not used a personal computer very much until they started using the Net. Their knowledge of Microsoft Windows was therefore minimal.

With my dear reviewers in mind – along with thousands of people like them – here are some pointers on Windows features that you need to understand to get the full benefit of the Net.

1. how to create a folder
A folder, called a directory in early versions of Windows, is a convenient place to store similar material you discover on the Net. To create a folder, in Windows Explorer, single click on an existing folder where you would like to place your new folder. Next, right click on a blank area, select **New**, **Folder**, and type in the name of the folder to replace the words **New Folder**.

2. how to find a file

In Windows Explorer select **Tools**, **Find**, **Files or Folders**. Here you can search for files by name, text in the tile or date the file was last saved. Figure 5.2 illustrates this procedure.

how to move a file into a new folder

Create a new folder using Windows Explorer as described in step 1. Locate the file you wish to move. If you need to find a file or folder, you can search for it using the steps explained in step 2 above. Once you locate the file, simply select it in the right pane and move it to the left pane. Figure 1 illustrates this procedure.

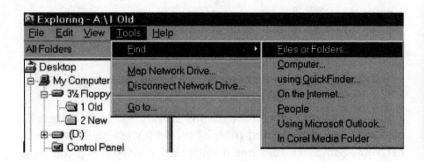

Figure 5.2 *Finding files using Internet Explorer*

there is plenty of truth in humour

Three engineers – an electrical engineer, a chemical engineer and a Microsoft engineer – are riding in a car. Suddenly the car stalls and stops by the side of the road. The three engineers look at each other with bewilderment, wondering what could be wrong.

Not knowing much about car mechanics, the electrical engineer suggests 'Let's strip down the electronics of the car and try to trace where a fault might have occurred.' Not knowing much about electronics, the chemical engineer suggests 'Maybe the fuel has become emulsified and is causing a blockage somewhere in the system.' The Microsoft engineer suggests 'Why don't we close all the windows, get out, get back in, and open all the windows? Maybe it'll work.'

Windows 98

Windows 98 is not radically different from Windows 95. Here are some of the features of this upgraded operating system.

compatibility with Windows 95
Microsoft claims there is complete compatibility with programs you run under Windows 95.

hardware requirements
If your current hardware runs Windows 95, it will run Windows 98 without upgrading. However, you may require new hardware to access some of the new features in Windows 98.

true Web integration
Every window acts like a Web page. Objects in windows open

with a single click, rather than with a double-click. You can activate the Explorer bar so you can jump backwards and forwards to various locations.

OnNow technology

If your hardware allows, Windows 98 shuts down the hard drive when it is not accessed for a period of time. Windows 98 'wakes up' when told you you or, for example, when there is an incoming fax call.

navigation improvements

With a single click, the new desktop icon minimizes and restores all open windows. You can create your own custom toolbars. You can place Desktop items on the Task Bar, thus eliminating the need to minimize windows to use a Desktop icon. The toolbars can be resized and rearranged.

improved start menu

Includes additional items on the **Find** command sub-menu and a command for Web Favorites (included in Internet Explorer 4 and later versions).

multimedia

There are more multimedia possibilities.

new peripherals

Windows 98 makes it easier to add new peripherals like scanners.

obtaining and using the latest versions of Net software

There is a good chance you received your first copy of Web software bundled with other programs. Microsoft's Internet Explorer is often bundled with other Microsoft products, such as Windows. Netscape Navigator™ is included with Corel products. At some time, however, you may wish to move up to an upgraded version of the software with more features. Here is a list of sources for some of the more common Web applications. If you are looking for others you could check out the search tool Yahoo! at *http://www.yahoo.com/* (also *http://uk.yahoo.com/*).

Microsoft's Internet Explorer
http://www.microsoft.com/ie/download/
When new versions appear, they are highlighted on the Web site. At other times, you will have to search to find the version you are seeking.

Netscape Navigator and other Netscape products such as Netscape Communicator
http://home.netscape.com/
This site also provided access to other Netscape products.

Eudora for e-mail
http://www.eudora.com/eudoralight/
You can download a complete manual for Eudora Light.

Pegasus Mail for e-mail
http://www.zdnet.co.uk/software/free/top/sw26.html
You can download Pegasus Mail at this site.

an aversion to new versions?

Maybe you know people who literally lined up to purchase the latest version of software. Next, they installed it and spent hours on the telephone with the product support people trying to deal with 'bugs' (programming errors or oversights that diminish the performance of the software). Perhaps you know people who installed a beta, or test version, of software and immediately had serious computer problems – now they swear they'll never do that again.

Producing software is a complex process, often requiring more time than estimated. Deadlines are missed and pressure mounts to release a product that is not fully tested. In that context, buyers must be wary.

Here are a few things you can do in deciding whether to use a new release of software.

checking out new releases of Web software

▓ Read reviews of software in Internet-based software magazines. You can search through back issues by using indexes that the editors have set up on the Net.

The search engine Yahoo! lists computer magazines at *http://www.yahoo.com/computers/* (also *http://uk. yahoo.com/*). Some of the more prominent sites are *http://www.zdnet.com/* (also *http://www.zdnet.co.uk/*) and *http://www.byte.com/*

▓ Use an Internet search engine like *http://www. lycos.com/* and *http://www.altavista.com/* (also *http:// www.altavista.co.uk/*).

You might find an independent evaluation that appeals to you, or find a discussion in a newsgroup that makes sense to you.

▓ Speak to your friends, or join a computer group where such topics are discussed.

Armed with this information, you will be able to ask pertinent questions and make an informed decision.

tooling your searches

There are more than 150 million Web pages. Undoubtedly, some of these contain information you could use in your work and play. But how do you find what you need? That is why we have search tools! (There is no charge for using the search tools described below.) Some of these tools like Yahoo! use human cataloguers to find, evaluate, select, and index links on the Internet. Other search engines send out small programs referred to as spiders, crawlers or indexers to review and catalog Web sites and copy text they find into a database. When a user of a search engine types in a phrase or keyword, the search engine scans the pages in its index for matches.

Here are some suggestions for using search tools.

read the site's 'how to use' section

No matter how wonderful a search tool is, you must use it the way it was designed to be used.

be precise

Be specific. This helps the engine pinpoint the most relevant documents. For example, if you want to find information about a film, search for the title of the film rather than the names of actors or producers.

be patient
You might have to try out a few different searches if your first attempts are unproductive.

check your spelling
It sounds obvious, but even the best spellers make mistakes.

use second-phrase searches
Some search tools have 'similar page' queries. These can lead you to similar Web pages.

use capitalization where necessary
Don't conduct a search on Bill Gates by typing 'bill gates' – a common error.

learn about Boolean operators
Boolean operators include AND, AND NOT, OR, and parentheses. To work, they must appear in ALL CAPS and with a space on each side. For example, 'x AND y' finds documents that contain both the words x and y.

behind the scenes of search tools

Here is a summary of a few of the many search tools available. Search tools also have information about advanced features that you might wish to check out if your initial searches do not produce results. Search tools are always updating their approaches, so some of the following information will change with time.

AltaVista

AltaVista searches by keywords and by phrases in quotation marks. It also offers several different ways to refine your search. Typically, AltaVista produces more matches than other search tools.

Excite

Excite searches for the exact words you type into the request area and for ideas closely related to those words. The Excite Search Wizard dynamically suggests words you may want to add to your search.

HotBot

In published reports, HotBot outperforms Excite, InfoSeek and AltaVista in speed and accuracy. HotBot spiders search the Web every two weeks to update their data.

InfoSeek

InfoSeek uses a natural-language query interface, and also conducts streamlined searches within the responses to your queries.

InfoSpace

InfoSpace is a leading search tool for Web sites, e-mail addresses, and old friends.

Lycos

Lycos is a search engine and a directory. It uses several different categories.

MetaCrawler

This search engine uses different tools such as AltaVista, Excite, Infoseek, Lycos, Webcrawler and Yahoo!

Yahoo!

Yahoo! relies on humans, not spiders to categorize information by topic. Yahoo! rolls over to other search engines if it can't provide a match.

The full URL, or universal resource locator, for these search tools includes the word name given above plus *http://www.* before the name, and an extension, normally *.com* or *.co.uk*, after the name. For example, the full address for AltaVista UK is *http://www.altavista.co.uk/* In current versions of Web browsers all you need to type in the location toolbar of your browser is the name of the tool (eg *altavista*), the software will automatically add the rest.

mission accomplished with a search

Complete the search described below to polish your skills. Here are the steps that I followed at the beginning of 2000. They will still work unless the ZDNet has been altered. Many people have good results finding useful software on the Web. So let's try it!

learning what is available in ZDNet

1. Open your browser. (I am using Netscape Navigator 4. You can use the browser you prefer.)
2. In your browser's location bar type 'zdnet.com'. In earlier versions of Netscape, and other browsers, you might have to type *http://zdnet.com* (Do not type a full stop after the 'com'.)
3. When the ZDNet site opens, select the word 'Downloads'. This will open up the ZDNet Downloads page.
4. In the query form type **track Internet usage**. Click on **S**earch.

5. The foregoing query generates a list of sites where you can download software. If you wish to download immediately, simply click on the underlined name of the software you prefer.

6. To learn more about the different software from magazine reviews before downloading, you can access the Web sites of computer magazines such as *http://www.zdnet.com/* (or *http://www.zdnet.co.uk/*) and *http://www.byte.com* Just type in the name of the software in the query form of the search tool.

making sense out of Net error messages

My colleague, Nancy, read about a terrific Web site in the morning paper. She immediately tried to access the site. Her browser returned the message: 'The server does not have a DNS entry.' In other words, the Web site did not exist. What could she do?

Here are a few thoughts on how to deal with Web access problems.

- After you type a URL in a browser's location toolbar, the browser returns an error message: 'The server does not have a DNS entry.' This means that your server did not locate the site you are searching for. This may be due to factors such as the connections between servers being too busy with other Internet traffic, or your having typed the URL incorrectly.

  Try again in case lines are busy.

  Check your spelling of the server name, revise if necessary, and try again.

  With a search tool, look up the name of the site. For example, in the Lycos query form, type in the name of the company or site you are searching for. This will find a new URL if the Webmaster has moved the site – a distinct possibility if the site is successful and has now established a new, trendy domain name.

▧ You type a URL in the location toolbar of your browser. Your browser unsuccessfully searches for a URL. You receive an error message: '404 File Not Found' or 'Not Found'.

This means your server located the site (the computer) that the URL is associated with but not your specific URL. You can try to change the ending of the URL, or go to a higher level of the Web site by shortening the URL. For example, if you searched for *netscape.com/downloads/* and got an error message, you could go back up to *http://netscape.com/* to see if there is a link to the resources you need or you could try typing 'download' instead of 'downloads.'

▧ Here are a few steps to take with all error messages.
- Read the message carefully.
- Relax. Tell yourself: error messages are part of using the Web.
- Repeat the action you did that led to the error message in the first place.
- If the message repeats itself, write it down. That way you will be able to spell out the nature of your problem to someone helping you.
- Check the basics. Are you hooked up? Did you type accurately?
- Try again.
- If the problem persists, check the notes in this manual; check the Web; decide if you need help.
- If you need help, call your ISP, a colleague, or a friend.
- Remain patient; you will solve your problem, and if you go about it systematically, you will also learn about the Net. That way, you will be able to deal with the problem faster if it happens again.

saving your Net treasures

You need information about the competition, a new market, a new product, new legislation, or whatever. You open your Web browser, select a search tool, use some clever techniques to pinpoint the information you need, and you find just what you want. What do you do next? You could print the information, but what if you lost your copy? Moreover, where would you file it? You could mark the site with an electronic bookmark using your browser. Then the next time you are on the Net you could access the site again. These are good ideas. While you are at it, why not save the file to your hard drive? If you save a page from the Web to your hard drive, you can access it later when you are not online, or send it via e-mail to a colleague or client. If you save your Net treasure as an HTML file, you or anyone else can view it anywhere in the world using a Web browser.

Here are a few questions and answer about saving treasures from the Web.

where do I save treasures I find on the Net?
Set up folders that explicitly describe the subject. You have 255 characters to do this. Two or three dozen should be plenty.

how do I save my treasures?
The same as saving a file in any Windows application. Use Ctrl + S.

what should I name the files?
Like setting up folders, you have 255 characters. You can use blank spaces to separate words in the file name.

what characters can I not use?
\ / : * ? " ' < > and I are forbidden.

what about extensions?
You can add a three-letter extension. Alternatively, you can let the software do it. It works well to let the software decide.

what about software files I download from the Net – things like the latest version of Netscape Communicator?
When you download files they have file names that only true computer whizzes will understand and remember. Use the other tips on this page to help you name files of software that you download. Give the folder and file a name that means something to you and you will be able to find it later. You can use descriptions, dates, numbers and any other conventions that make sense to you.

how do I find the files after saving them?
If you are looking for files you worked with recently, Windows offers the last 15 in the **Documents** section on the **Start** menu. Stay alert when using this list. It may not include all files if you have had a computer crash. **Find** on the **Start** menu will also help locate a folder or a file.

keyboard shortcuts

For some users, a mouse is a handy gadget that makes it possible to navigate the Net. However, if you are looking for ways to enhance your productivity with the Net you should investigate keyboard shortcuts.

For example, you want to compose an e-mail message. In Netscape Messenger, you move the mouse pointer to **Message** and select **New Message**. A faster way is to hold down the **Ctrl** key and select the **M** key. This is written as **Ctrl + M**. This shortcut performs the same action with one step, compared to several steps with the mouse.

If the shoulder of your 'mousing' arm becomes sore it could be that you have the debilitating condition called 'mouse shoulder'. One of the best precautions to take against mouse shoulder or steps to take after you have it is to use keyboard shortcuts instead of your mouse.

The Web site of the library of the University of California, Riverside, gives simple steps for using computers more comfortably. The URL is *http://library.ucr.edu/~pflowers/ ergolib.html*

The table on the next page is a job aid to help you learn keyboard shortcuts. You should keep a copy close to your computer while you are learning these simple shortcuts.

windows keyboard shortcuts

Select	And you will...
Alt + F4	exit the current program.
Alt + Tab	switch to the previous application.
Alt + Tab + Tab	scroll through the list of open software applications.
Ctrl + Esc	show the start up menu and task bar if it is hidden.
Ctrl + A	select all the text and graphics in the document on the screen.
Ctrl + C	copy the selected area.
Ctrl + P	print the document on the screen.
Ctrl + S	save the document on the screen.
Ctrl + V	paste or insert the text you have copied or cut.
Ctrl + X	cut (remove) the selected text.
Ctrl + Z	undo the previous action.
Del	delete the selected area or the single closest character to the right.
Esc	close a dialog box.
F1	get help in a program or dialog box.
Shift + F10	view a shortcut menu for a selected item or area; next you can use your down arrow to select an item. This gives you access to the right mouse button features without touching the mouse!

12

Help is on the way

Do you use all of the **Help** that is available? Using **Help** will increase your knowledge of the Web and make it possible for you to be independent in your pursuit of Net knowledge.

how to access **H**elp resources in Windows

Help on the taskbar

Select **Help** on the taskbar start menu. Select the **Contents** menu (see Figure 12.1).

The items listed in Figure 12.1 provide critical Net information to help you get started.

wizards

Select **Help** in the taskbar's start menu. In the **Contents** menu, select **Troubleshooting**.

If you have trouble using the Internet, wizards provide step-by-step advice.

Figure 12.1 *Help in Windows*

Web Tutorial

Select **Help** on the Internet Explorer menu bar. Select **Web Tutorial** (see Figure 12.2).

This comprehensive review ranges from simple to complex. Internet connection is required.

help on Help

Select **Help** in the taskbar of Internet Explorer. Select **Index**.

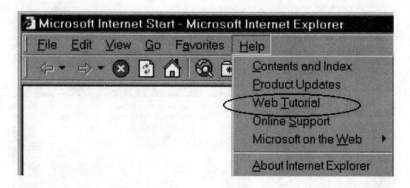

Figure 12.2 *Accessing the Web tutorial in Internet Explorer*

Type in **Help** and select **Display**. A list of many **Help** functions will appear.

You can customize **Help**, set bookmarks, add notes, and generally make **Help** part of your daily use of the Internet.

Help: seeing is believing, doing is understanding

Maybe you tried **Help**, did not find what you wanted and gave up in frustration. Try again. You will be amazed at the richness of the resources listed in **Help**. Take a test drive. Choose something you would like to learn more about. For example, select **Help** on the taskbar's Start Menu. Select the **Find** tab. Type in one word for the topic that interests you. Type 'help' for example. If you type '**Help**', several topics appear (the number will depend on the software you have loaded on your computer). You can select the ones that interest you and learn more and see the richness of the online **Help** resources. Figure 12.3 shows the **Help** topics dialog box open and the results of the steps described above.

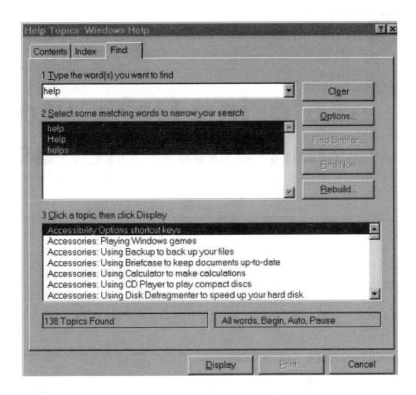

Figure 12.3   *Using the find tab to list help items*

exploring Help and pull-down menus

Help files provide answers to most, but not all, questions. A good way to fill in the gaps in Help is to study the menus and dialog boxes in your software and find your answers that way.

Here are a few ideas on using Help and menus to learn about e-mail software.

to set up a signature block that is automatically placed at the end of every e-mail you send.

Outlook Express: select Help, Contents and Index, and Search, type **signature** in the box, and then select the List Topics button.

Another way to obtain the same information is to: select Help, Help Contents, Index in the menu on the left, Address book cards in the list that appears, Creating a personal card.

Any of the Netscape Communicator applications: select Help, Help Contents, Index in the menu on the left, Signature, plain-text, Setting Mail & Group Preferences for your Identity.

to check you in-box for messages with a specific word in them

Outlook Express: look under **<u>E</u>dit**, and **<u>F</u>ind Message**.

Navigator Messenger: look under **<u>E</u>dit**, and **<u>S</u>earch Messages**.

shortcuts for adding names to your address book

Outlook Express: to place people automatically in your address book look under **<u>H</u>elp, <u>C</u>ontents, Tips and Tricks, Add contacts to your address book**.

Netscape Messenger: look under **<u>H</u>elp**. There is plenty of information about adding a name to your address book, but no reference to the right mouse key shortcut. Try this, in Netscape Messenger. With the **Inbox open** or with an incoming e-mail open, select your right mouse button.

steps in exploring <u>H</u>elp and pull-down menus

In the previous exercise, you dug into **<u>H</u>elp** and menus to find answers to questions about your e-mail software. The list below shows the steps you followed to perform the different activities.

to set up a signature block that is automatically placed at the end of every e-mail you send

Outlook Express: select **<u>T</u>ools, <u>S</u>tationery, <u>M</u>ail, Signature**, and complete the **Signature** dialog box.

Netscape Messenger: select **<u>E</u>dit, <u>P</u>references**. Select **<u>M</u>ail & Groups, Identity**, and **Edit Card**. Fill in your data, including the **Contact** tab.

Nescape Messenger: using a text editor like Wordpad or Notepad: prepare a file with the text you want in your message and save it in an easy-to-find folder with an easy-to-remember name like 'signature for e-mail in Messenger'. You must save it as a text document or '.txt' file. Open Netscape Communicator, select **Edit**, **Preferences**, **Mail & Groups**, **Identity**, **Signature File**, and **Choose**. Find the file you saved and select **Open**. In the **Preferences** select **OK**.

to check out your in-box for messages with a specific word in them

Outlook Express: select **Edit**, **Find Message**. Complete the **Find Message** dialog box.

Navigator Messenger: select **Edit**, search **Messages**, and fill in the **Search Messages** dialog box. (Remember, if you want to search in the body of the messages, you must select **Body**.)

shortcuts for adding names to your address book

Outlook Express: select **Tools** and **Address Book**, and complete the **Windows Address Book** dialog box. To place names automatically in the address book, select **Options**, **General** and place a check beside **Automatically**.

Navigator Messenger: In the **Inbox**, select the message with the e-mail address that you would like to add. Click on your right mouse button. Select **Add to Address Book**.

freeing space on your hard drive

Current hard drives seem unbelievably huge. You might wonder how anyone would ever run out of space on a hard drive that holds gigabytes of information? Given that new versions of software tie up huge blocks of disk space, running out of disk space may one day become a concern for you. The problem does not start with the Internet, but your Net software does contribute to it. For example, new versions of software from Nescape and Microsoft are disk-space-hungry. Netscape Communicator includes Navigator (browser), Messenger (e-mail), Collabra Discussion Groups (newsreader), Page Composer (basic tools for creating Web pages), Netcaster (tools for the automatic delivery of Web pages to you), and other minor applications.

Here are some easy-to-follow steps to clean up your drive.

■ *Discard old e-mail messages.*
This includes cleaning out the trash folder containing messages you have previously deleted.

■ *Delete the old Windows temporary files that collect on your computer.*
My temporary files are stored under Windows/temp and they end in '.tmp'. While you are in your temp

folder, you may delete other files too. However, don't delete today's temporary files. Remember, deleting files this way moves them to the recycle bin. To remove these files from your hard drive, and free up space, you need to empty your recycle bin.

■ *Delete items from the recycle bin. This is final, so check for gems before deleting.*

There might be a few hundred files in your recycle bin – up to 10 per cent of your hard drive space. On your desktop, click on the Recycle Bin icon. View the file names. To permanently delete everything, select **File** and **Empty Recycle Bin**.

■ *Optimize your hard drive so that sections of electronic files are stored beside each other.*

Open the **Start** menu on the task bar. Select **Programs**. Select **Accessories**, **System Tools**, and **Disk Defragmenter**. The defragmenter will conduct a fragmentation test on your drive and recommend what you should do.

■ *Set up folders strategically.*

If you set up folders strategically, it will make it easier to clean up your hard drive. For example, you can set up a folder that you call 'dump' and in it place zipped files that you download from the Net. Once you have executed these files, you can delete the original zipped files that you downloaded. Of course, if you have plenty of disk drive space, you might prefer to save these files in case you need them later. But placing them in a dump folder (and possibly clearly named sub-folders within the dump folder) helps you sort the grain from the chaff.

■ *Delete temporary files that your browser creates.*

On my computer Netscape Navigator automatically stores files in a folder at c:/Windows/Temp/**Temporary Internet Files**. The large number of files that are stored in this folder might surprise you.

using the Net proactively

A proactive person takes responsibility for his or her actions and makes things happen. A proactive Net user discovers how the Net functions, keeps references handy, and uses them to help solve problems. For example, a proactive Net user sets up e-mail so it is easy to manage incoming and outgoing messages.

Use the following checklist to determine whether you are using the Net in a proactive manner.

Proactive quality	I do this
When I have a question about using my Net software, I check out **Help**.	**Always Sometimes Never**
I organize my bookmarks of good Web sits and use them later.	**Always Sometimes Never**
I use the address book and group mailing feature to save time when addressing e-mail.	**Always Sometimes Never**

Proactive quality	I do this
I go to software providers' sites and learn about new software.	**Always Sometimes Never**
When I use a search tool to do complex searches and I am not certain what to do, I check how to conduct advanced searches.	**Always Sometimes Never**
When I am searching for information, I do not let myself get sidetracked.	**Always Sometimes Never**
Before starting an Internet search, I think through what I need.	**Always Sometimes Never**
I use reference materials such as online manuals to help solve problems.	**Always Sometimes Never**
I have set up my e-mail so it is easy to manage incoming and outgoing messages.	**Always Sometimes Never**
When I compose e-mail messages, I am not connected to my ISP and in that way I do not waste hook-up time.	**Always Sometimes Never**
If I have a large file to send over the Net, I use WinZip®.	**Always Sometimes Never**
I store Net information in clearly worded folders.	**Always Sometimes Never**
I delete old Net files in my e-mail and browser software.	**Always Sometimes Never**

Congratulations if most of your answers were in the 'always' box. If you did not do as well as you would like, you can start today to be more proactive.

chat, newsgroups, e-mail and mailing lists

Chat, newsgroups, e-mail and mailing lists are Internet communication services. They are grouped together in this section because of their similar purposes – to put people in touch with each other via the Net. Newgroups, e-mail mailing lists and sometimes chat are governed by a code of conduct called 'netiquette'. The users of these services are expected to follow these rules. In addition, there are some similarities in the software you use in newsgroups, e-mail and mailing lists.

Newsgroups, mailing lists, e-mail and chat exist to send and receive messages over the Net. A main difference is that in e-mail you normally send messages to individuals or small groups, while in newsgroups you post messages to a group. Similarly in a mailing list you send messages to a computer, which in turn sends them to members of a group. Consequently, you might be sending a message to thousands of people when you post a message to a newsgroup or a mailing list. There are over 30,000 newsgroups and over 80,000 mailing lists.

Chat is the most distinctive of these four Net communications services. In chat, you use special software to send real-time messages to both individuals and groups. Typically, chat is also different in that participants assume nicknames – such as 'Fat Cat' and 'Truffles.' Masquerading in chat produces some entertaining sessions. But beware: what you say in chat may be read by many people. And what you say in chat and in the other three services explained in this section can be traced.

Not all chat sessions are dedicated to frivolity. I know, for example, people who use chat software and the services of ICQ (pronounced I seek you) to carry on serious business discussion and develop training materials with people from around the world.

Some of us have trouble imagining life before e-mail and other Internet communication services. Enthusiasts use these four services to communicate with colleagues, friends, and family scattered around the world. They, or I should say we, also use these services to identify clients and to communicate with people with similar interests, globally.

For others, communicating on the Net is a royal pain. They complain that there is too much junk e-mail, too many instant experts pontificating unfounded opinions, and too much volume. Others say that such Internet services have divided the rich, who have access, from the poor, who are cut off from the Internet.

Let's take a closer look at chat, newsgroups, e-mail and mailing lists, trying to eliminate the pain and increase the gain. Along the line you will begin to, as one of my friends says, 'manage the e-mail monster.'

the chatter about chat

Chat has become synonymous for cultivating online romances. Sorry, I can't help you there. My interest is in explaining how you can use chat to enhance your productivity at home and in the office.

Here are a few facts about chat and suggestions on how you might use it.

how do I sign up for chat?

If you subscribe to America Online (AOL) or another value-added ISP, you have your own chat group and software. Other people rely on Internet Relay Chat (IRC) and other software to help them locate chat sessions. ICQ ('I Seek You') is a chat program that lets you communicate online with your friends and business colleagues. You create a contact list containing only people you want to communicate with. You can send them messages, chat with them, swap files, and more. You can obtain ISQ software at *http://www.icq.com/*

what do I need to participate in chat sessions?

The first thing you need is software. You can obtain mIRC at *http://www.mirc.co.uk/*

where can I use chat?

The mIRC Web site has plenty of information and links to chat sites. The best way to learn is 'by doing' – by joining a chat group. Sites designated for beginners are a good place to start. Before you launch into chat you should check the file called **Readme.txt** and the help file of your chat software.

how can I use chat for business?

IRC can host your business meetings. Although the business possibilities of chat are not fully exploited, Yahoo! and other search tools provide information about chat sites for business and other interests.

You can record below information you have collected about other chat users, chat rooms and sources of chat information, along with other information (such as your 'handle').

_____

_____

_____

_____

_____

_____

_____

_____

_____

the scoop on newsgroups

Contrary to what their name implies, newsgroups do not bring you the daily news. They might be better named discussion groups or special interest groups, because members of newsgroups explore a specified topic. Nomenclature is evolving, however, and newsgroups are called discussion groups and discussion forums in the Netscape Communicator <u>H</u>elp file.

Newsgroups, like chat groups and mailing lists, are ways to organize Internet communication. If you need information on a subject, newsgroups might be your best bet for posting your query. The subject areas of newsgroups are vast, so chances are one deals with your subject of interest.

Here are a few answers to common questions about newsgroups.

what is a newsgroup?

A newsgroup is part of a worldwide discussion system called Usenet. Newsgroup names are classified hierarchically by subject. 'Articles' or 'messages' are 'posted' to these newsgroups by people using computers with the appropriate software. These articles are next broadcast to other interconnected computer systems via the Internet. There are over 30,000 newsgroups listed at *http://www.liszt.com/*

what do I need to participate in a newsgroup?

You will probably find the software you need to access news-groups bundled with your Internet browser. In Netscape it is called **Collabra Discussion Groups**. Your ISP needs to link to the newsgroup you have selected before you can have access to them.

how do I select a newsgroup?

Your newsreader probably has a list of newsgroups. To learn how newsgroups function in Netscape's Collabra, check out **Help, Collabra**. Here you will learn how to identify groups available to you and how to subscribe to or view discussions by selecting **File, Subscribe to Discussion Groups**.

how can I use newsgroups for business?

You need to review the list of newsgroups provided by your ISP. Make a selection of groups that seem promising and check them out. See the preceding item for more information on selecting newsgroups.

Search for more information about newsgroups and groups in your areas of interest at *http://www.faqs.org/*

You can record below information you have collected about newsgroups.

Name	Activity	Comments

mastering e-mail

which e-mail software will it be?

Have you ever wished you knew whether an e-mail message you sent had been opened at the other end? Ever wished you could have multiple e-mail accounts on one computer so that replies to your e-mail would be separated from messages sent to other people using the same computer?

The chart on page 52 lists a few e-mail features for you to investigate. Products change, so you should check Web sites and magazines for the latest specs. For example, find out about the new features of Netscape by searching in an online magazine such as we find in ZDNet's Software Library at *http://www.zdnet.com/* (or *http://www.zdnet.co.uk/*).

If these features sound enticing, you should contact your ISP or your office technical service group for advice. Ask which e-mail software they support and why, and if you obtain new e-mail software, will they help you set it up.

Features	Software with the features	Costs
Learn if your e-mail has been opened at the receiving computer. (May require that the receiver of the e-mail message is using the same software.)	Pegasus Outlook 2000	Pegasus is freeware – not shareware – use it without charge, on as many servers and machines as you wish. Netscape Messenger is currently available on the Net. Outlook 2000 comes with your purchase of Microsoft Office 2000.
Create individual accounts with separate passwords and in-boxes.	Pegasus and Netscape Messenger allow for this.	
Automatically put names of senders of incoming e-mail in your address book.	Nescape Messenger in Communicator 4 has this feature.	
Spell check the e-mail messages you compose.	Pegasus and Netscape Messenger have this feature and Outlook 2000 can be configured to provide it through your word processor.	

saving time and money with e-mail attachments

I praise e-mail every time I successfully send files to a client or colleague as an attachment to an e-mail message. Using attachments, consultants can send final reports to clients, and authors can send articles and book drafts to publishers. It is fast, inexpensive, and relatively simple – if you know how. Here are some tips to help you.

how do I send an electronic file with an e-mail message?
In Netscape Messenger, select Ctrl + M, **File**, **Attach**, **File**, and select the name of the file.

you receive an e-mail message indicating there is a file attached. You do not know what to do.

In Netscape Messenger, just click on the paper clip image or the clickable area that appears on the bottom of your page.

someone sends you a file attached to an e-mail message. It does not arrive as a separate file. Instead it is in the body of the e-mail message and it is garbled.

There are at least four options. Call a techie for help. Communicate with the person who sent you the file and set up your software to communicate better with each other. Use a decoder program, available on the Net, to unscramble the message. Have the sender cut and paste the text of the file into a new e-mail message.

you have a large file to send. You would like to attach it to an e-mail message, but it will use several minutes of your expensive hook-up time. The person receiving the message will also need to stay hooked-up for a lengthy period of time to download your message.

You can make the file smaller by compressing, or zipping it. You will need the software to compress your file and the recipient will need the same or similar software to unzip or decompress the file you send. You can also combine several files into one and make self-extracting files. WinZip is an excellent zip utility.

don't leave home without e-mail access

For many people, e-mail is an essential tool of their work. Checking e-mail several times a day has become a normal part of their work routine. What happens when hooked-up people are working out of town, are at a conference or, dare I say, on a holiday?

Rather than carting around a laptop and hooking up to one of the Internet services, you might find it more convenient to configure another desktop computer to receive your e-mail. Bill did it recently at a cybercafe and his e-mail came so quickly that the owner did not charge him. Another time, Mary was attending a conference and computers were set up for participants to experience the Web. Mary found it was a snap to use these computers to download her e-mail. Another time Allan was visiting his family in Switzerland and, with a few changes to their computer, he was able to retrieve all the e-mail from his US account.

It is simply a matter of setting the host computer to receive the mail from your e-mail account. You do not need to dial long distance to your ISP or your home computer. Follow these steps to receive your e-mail on another computer.

1. Get permission to download your e-mail. Some people have a phobia about others touching their computers, so please be careful.
2. To be on the safe side, the first time you set up someone else's computer to receive your e-mail, do it with the help of a techie.
3. Explain what you are about to do, why, how, and what's in it for the other person. Show them how to do it and they can use the same technique when they travel.
4. Note very clearly the current settings that you will modify.
5. After you get your e-mail, be certain to reset the computer to its original settings.

Here are the basic steps for configuring someone else's computer to receive your e-mail.

In Netscape take the following steps:

1. From any of the programs in the Netscape Communicator suite, select **C**ommunicator.
2. Select **M**essenger Mailbox.
3. Under **E**dit, select **P**references.
4. Select **Mail Server** (see Figure 19.1, below).
5. Revise to reflect your parameters. You can note these in the table on page 9, if you have not already done so.
6. Click OK and check for messages as you would normally do on your own computer.

Other ways to access your e-mail while you travel include the following. Subscribe to an Internet service provider that has access phone numbers in several centres. Or visit the site *http://www.mailstart.com/* (or *http://www.mailstart.co.uk/*) and preview your e-mail. You can set up a free Web-based e-mail account at most Web search engines and at *http://www.mailcity.lycos.com/* These services are accessible from any computer with an Internet connection.

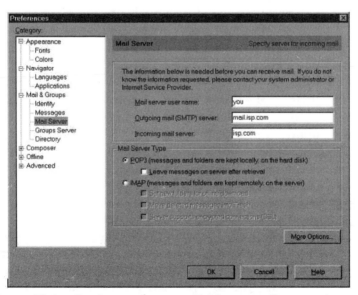

Figure 19.1 *Setting preferences in Netscape Communicator*

mastering business rules for e-mail

E-mail is a very powerful business tool. A client asks for information and you can have it sitting in his or her e-mail in-basket in minutes – anywhere in the world! You can electronically staple attachments to your e-mail, and use e-mail to send self-running presentations, demonstration software, and even 30-day trial versions of software you are distributing.

Here is some advice to help you get the most out of e-mail in a business context.

- Check your e-mail regularly. This gives the impression you are available and eager to serve.
- Respond to messages as they come in. This gives the impression you are accessible.
- Give an interim reply if necessary. This gives the impression you are treating the question seriously.
- Spell check your e-mail. This gives the impression that you provide or produce a quality product.
- Set up an automated signature block at the bottom with all your contact information. This gives the impression that you welcome contact in other media, by telephone, fax, or snail mail – your postal service.
- Perform a virus scan on files you attach to e-mail. Sending someone a file with a virus leaves a very bad impression.
- Remember e-mail is not particularly private. If you err in addressing your message, who knows who will get it. Although people on the Net are forgiving to newbies, a foul-up like this is embarrassing, to say the least.
- Don't use a smiley (eg :-)) in your business mail. :-) It is cute but not business-like.
- When replying to an e-mail message, include key text

from the message to which you are replying. This makes it clear which topics you are addressing.

▩ When commenting on another message and not using the reply feature, use the same subject heading as the message you received. This will help senders who use their e-mail software to sort their messages by subject.

getting advice from mailing lists

This is a true story. George had purchased a new laptop computer. He loaded it to make a PowerPoint presentation. The next time he tried to boot up his new technological marvel, nothing worked. Using another computer, George posted a quick message to a mailing list, asking members for help. Fortunately another member of the list with a similar computer was able to guide George. Within 30 minutes, George was able to use his laptop to make his presentation.

You too, could have your questions answered on a mailing list. Here's how to get started.

what are mailing lists?
Mailing lists are dynamic meeting places for the exchange of ideas, opinions, and information. Subscribers to mailing lists help other members solve problems, obtain information, and make contacts. Mailing lists are sometimes called listservs, e-mail lists and electronic mailing lists.

how do I learn about mailing lists?
You can learn about 80,000 mailing lists at *http://www.liszt. com*

how do mailing lists work?

You locate a list that interests you and join, or 'subscribe.' Initially, you will normally receive administrative information from the list. Retain this information. It tells you how to sign off and other important things. You will begin to receive messages posted to the list. If you like, you can send questions in the form of an e-mail message to the address of the list. Members decide if they wish to answer your question. They may answer you individually or to the list, in which case all members may receive a copy.

how do I join a mailing list?

If the 'listserv' program runs the list, join by sending an e-mail message to the administrative address with the following: Subscribe, your last name, your first name. If your mail list server software is 'Majordomo', do not include your name in the subscribing or quitting messages.

what do I do when I join a list?

Read the joining instructions and features of your list. How does it work? Will postings be screened? What specific rules of netiquette does the list have, if any? What are the rules about advertising? What are the objectives of the list? What are the delivery options? How do you change them? Are there archives? Introduce yourself to the group. Normally members expect a short biography of no more than 20 lines.

what is lurking?

Lurking means to join a mailing list, to receive messages, to read them but not to reply. Lurking is acceptable behaviour. In fact, in some large lists there are too many members to permit active participation by more than a small percentage of members. So there are plenty of lurkers.

netiquette for newsgroups and mailing lists

Participants in newsgroups and mailing lists sometimes criticize each other for the messages they post. As a member of mailing lists and newsgroups, I am amazed at the amount of acrimonious debate resulting when people do not follow rules such as those listed below. The rules of netiquette are standard and any group you join will have similar ones. If you follow these rules you will not be criticized, or flamed, by fellow subscribers to a list or newsgroup.

Here are some netiquette rules for newsgroups, mailing lists, and even e-mail.

- Never send any messages that you would not mind seeing on the evening news.
- Avoid capitalizing since this is generally termed SHOUTING!
- Include your signature at the bottom of messages and your other contact information. (Use the automatic signature feature.)

■ Keep paragraphs and messages short and to the point.

■ Always include a pertinent subject title for the message. This way recipients can locate the message quickly in their inbox.

■ Do not use sarcasm, rudeness (flames), or complex humour. Without face to face communication, your joke may be viewed as criticism.

■ Remember: mailing lists have worldwide membership. Do not assume that people will understand your reference to TV, sport, pop culture, or current events in your country.

■ Follow all guidelines that the list owner has posted as local netiquette standards for the list.

■ Find out if there is a FAQ for a group that you have joined. (A FAQ, which stands for Frequently Asked Questions, is a record of key information about questions that members typically ask – and answers.) Read the FAQ. Try to use it to answer your questions. Veteran members get annoyed when they see the same questions being raised on the list every few weeks.

■ When replying to a question asked by another subscriber, make it clear to which element of the posting you are replying.

■ Follow the rules set by the list owner for spreading your commercial message.

■ Send personal notes to individuals, not to the list.

■ Avoid posting 'me too' messages.

■ When asking fellow members for help, a good approach is to ask them to reply to you personally. When you have several replies, you can post them to all members of the list, thereby cutting down on the number of messages received by every member of the list.

intranets for business

Businesses and other large organizations use intranets to help achieve their goals. What I have said about Internet software also applies to intranets, since they use the same software and general approach.

grasping intranet basics

Intranet. Internet. They sound similar, but are they?

what are intranets?
Intranets are like the Internet, but within an organization. Using popular Internet software, like Internet Explorer or Netscape Navigator, an intranet allows people to communicate as they do on the Internet.

what are the benefits of an intranet?
With an intranet, your organization can distribute information dynamically. Click and employees check out data in the annual report, read the new policy on parental leave, or check out the latest list of training courses on how to use the Net.

what is the difference between the two?

An intranet is normally not open to the public, unless it is linked to the Internet. The Internet is generally open to the public, although you can set passwords to control entry to an Internet site, too.

is an intranet connected to the Internet?

An intranet does not need to be connected to the Internet. Security can be an issue here. If your intranet is connected to the Internet, you can send e-mail to anyone who is also connected to the Internet.

what are the advantages of intranets?

Intranet documents are more dynamic, more engaging than their paper-based counterparts. Multimedia intranet documents include pictures, sounds, videos, and text. Also, on your organization's intranet, different types of computers can communicate with each other. Intranets are generally simple to set up and run.

what are the challenges of intranets?

The downside of running an intranet is that multimedia requires robust hardware.

where can I see an intranet in action?

You can see an intranet in action and track a Federal Express package at *http://www.fedex.com/* To find a zip code in the US Postal Service, view *http://www.usps.gov/*

are intranets effective for delivering training?

Placing documents on an intranet can help and encourage wider distribution. However, the effectiveness of the training material, as always, depends on how well it is designed. Are needs clearly defined and addressed? Do the materials deal with real, practical situations? These are some of the issues that determine whether training materials are effective.

put people in touch using an intranet

Here are five ways to put people in touch using an intranet.

▥ *Communication* – E-mail distributes information and provides a channel for people to discuss the information.

For example, a mailing list can be set up for employees to exchange views on an issue.

▥ *Online reference* – You can create an online library of hyperlinked information and files for downloading.

Course catalogs, schedules, and other materials can be distributed via your intranet.

▥ *Registration and ordering* – Recent versions of word processors can be used to create forms that users can complete online.

Using such forums, employees can register for training.

▥ *Distribution of Web-based information* – File Transfer Protocol (FTP), an easy-to-use service of the Internet, can be used to allow users to download materials.

For instance, participants in a training programme can download Web-based training (WBT) modules.

▥ *Delivery of Web-based training modules* – Add-ons and plug-ins, tools such as Shockwave, Flash, JAVA, ActiveX and others can be used to deliver real time WBT.

As a result, classroom training can be replaced with WBT, or a combination of the two can be used.

intranets are cost effective

Looking for ways to cut the cost of doing business? Intranet-based information dissemination may save money because:

■ HTML, the universal programming language of the Web, is economical to use. You only need to program once for use on all platforms such as Windows, Macintosh, UNIX, and others.

■ Placing information materials on a main computer that feeds others (a server) cuts printing costs and distribution time.

■ Placing information materials on a main computer permits quick access and economical updating.

■ The intranet technology is readily available and economical to purchase, compared to other technologies such as CD ROM, video, and computer-based training.

■ The same software is used for accessing an intranet as is used for the Internet. Therefore, users who are familiar with Internet software for browsing and e-mail can readily learn to use an organization's intranet.

■ The ease of setting up intranets, by using HTML tags, allows many groups in an organization to have an intranet presence and identity.

■ The popularity of HTML and the Web has led software producers to incorporate HTML conversion programs in common software like word processors, presentation graphics, spreadsheets and databases. In effect, all you need to do is prepare your document in your regular software and select one command to convert it to a Web document. Adding links is also relatively easy to do.

■ Software called add-ons can be used by a browser on an intranet to add multimedia sound and graphics.

browsing information about intranets and the Internet

The Net is the best place to learn about Net subjects such as software, security and new technologies. Here is a list of Web sites about intranets and the Internet. The descriptive texts listed below are quoted directly from the Web sites. Web sites are extremely dynamic and, as a result, some of the following sites may move or change over a period of time.

BBC Online
News, background, interesting features.
  http://www.bbc.co.uk/

December Communications, Inc
Reports about people, events, technology, public policy, culture, practices, study, and applications related to human communication and interaction in online environments.
  http://www.december.com/

e-learning hub.com
A comprehensive service about e-learning founded by Brooke Broadbent.
http://www.e-learninghub.com/

E-newsletters at internet.com
Subscribe to newsletters about news, resources, stocks, e-commerce, software and to country-specific electronic newsletters.
http://e-newsletters.internet.com/

Inside Training Technology
A free magazine about technology-based training available on the Web.
http://www.ittrain.com/

Intranet Design Magazine
An online resource for people starting and managing intranets and other networks. Includes current news, articles on key topics and a glossary of terms.
http://idm.internet.com/

Intranet Journal
Read the latest intranet news and find out what's happening in the world of intranet and extranet solutions.
http://www.intranetjournal.com/

LondonTown.com
Extensive information about activities in London. For tourists and residents. What is happening.
http://www.londontown.com/

Newmedia.com
Provides up-to-date information about business, design and technology.
http://www.newmedia.com/

Open University
Information about this leading institution with 160,000 graduates in the UK, Europe and many other countries.
http://www.open.ac.uk/

T.H.E. Journal

Your source for exploring Technological Horizons in Education!
News on the world of computers and related technologies, focusing
on applications that improve teaching and learning for all ages.

http://www.thejournal.com/

The Times and The Sunday Times

Provides links from each day's news and feature articles to related
events. It has a detailed archive of material for background and
research. Provides up-to-date news throughout the day. Even
previews the next day's edition.

http://www.the-times.co.uk/
http://www.sunday-times.co.uk/

Training SuperSite Publications Center

Here you can preview our award-winning publications and learn
more about the resources we offer to help you and your people do
their jobs more effectively. Each month, *Training* magazine delivers
an on-the-mark blend of provocative profiles, perceptive trend
stories, practical case studies, 'how-tos', special reports – all designed
to help you and your people do their jobs more effectively. Covers all
aspects of training, management, and organizational development,
motivation and performance improvement... Make your presentations more powerful with monthly how-to-topics, techniques, new
technologies, case studies, and more. Each month, Presentations
brings you the expert intelligence you need to make better presentations and more cost-effective decisions about the products you select.
Articles cover topics such as: 101 topics for better presentations,
creating a home page, presentation disasters and how to avoid them,
digital storing solutions, and much more.

http://www.trainingsupersite.com/pubset.htm

Vnunet.com

A comprehensive Web site serving several European markets with
computer news, products and jobs.

http://www.vnunet.com/

Webwise from the BBC

Practical tips on using the Web.

http://www.bbc.co.uk/webwise/

Wired Magazine

Wired Magazine charts the impact of technology on business, culture, life. We're more than a magazine. Wired offers everything from cutting-edge books to around-the-clock digital news, and from the world's best search engine to the Web's hottest sites.

http://www.wired.com/wired/

Yahoo! UK and Ireland

An extensive index of Web-based resources in the UK and Ireland. Includes information about Arts & Humanities, Business & Economy, Computers & Internet, Education, Entertainment, Government, Health, News & Media, Recreation & Sport, Reference, Regional, Science, Social Science, Society & Culture, and breaking news.

http://uk.yahoo.com/

You can record below the URLs of Web sites you identified through browsing sites listed above.

---

netting software for your intranet site

Browsers are fine for viewing text, but add-on programs are required to make browsers capable of delivering multimedia. Here is information about some of the more common free add-on programs that bring multimedia and other features to the Web.

Adobe Acrobat Reader

The PDF or portable document format files generated by Adobe Acrobat can be read on your Windows operating system, Macintosh, UNIX, and other systems – when they are equipped with the Adobe Acrobat Reader. This means that all computers see virtually the same images, independent of the operating system and word processor used to generate the file.

http://www.adobe.com/ (or *http://www.adobe.co.uk/*)

ActiveX

A Microsoft plug-in that brings multimedia to Internet Explorer.

http://www.microsoft.com/

Apple QuickTime

Running under Windows as well as the Macintosh environment, QuickTime brings animation, audio, music, MIDI and video to your screen.

http://www.apple.com.quicktime/

RealAudio

With this plug-in installed in your Netscape browser, you can listen to live and on-demand audio over the Internet using your standard modem.

http://www.realaudio.com/

Shockwave (sometimes called Macromedia Shockwave)

This is the most popular plug-in for viewing multimedia.

http://www.macromedia.com/shockwave

Netscape has a site that will help you select and download the latest plug-ins. For more information, use Netscape Navigator 4 to select **Help**, and **About Plug-ins**.

You can record below the URLs of Web sites for add-ons or other information you wish to note about add-ons.

_____

_____

_____

_____

_____

_____

_____

_____

exploring features in Internet Explorer 5

When new software hits the marketplace, consumers often wonder if they should shell out additional money for more features. If the software is free, like browsers from Microsoft and Netscape, then you don't have to consider your wallet. There are still the questions of whether the new software will run on your present system, whether it will be difficult to learn the new features, and if it is worth while to learn the new features. The following information will help you decide about moving up to Internet Explorer 5.

will my present hardware run Internet Explorer 5?
If you have been successfully running Internet Explorer 4 or an equivalent program, chances are your present system will run Internet Explorer 5.

what's new in Internet Explorer 5?
Internet Explorer 5 looks very much like Internet Explorer 4, since most of the new features are hidden. However, as Web sites start using these new features (eg virtual reality), they will become more apparent.

are the new features worth the effort of downloading them?

As more and more Web sites start using the new features in Internet Explorer 5, it will become increasingly important to upgrade.

featuring Internet Explorer

Perhaps you have courageously installed Internet Explorer and would like to learn to use its new features. Here are some thumbnail instructions. Look for more instructions under **Help** in Internet Explorer.

to conduct searches quickly

Go to the **Address** bar and type **go, find,** or **?**, followed by the topic you want information about. For example, type 'go Microsoft' in the address toolbar and a search tool will create a list of clickable URLs. If you are not online, Microsoft Connection Manager will dial for you.

to save keystrokes in the address bar

If you have visited a site recently, start to type the URL in the address toolbar. Internet Explorer completes the URL. Press **Enter** and the Web page you are seeking will open. For example, if you type **mi**, Internet Explorer 4 or 5 will complete the URL for the last Microsoft site you visited.

to glance at recently visited sites

Select **View, Explorer** bar, **History,** and use the menu to see pages you have visited for the previous several days and weeks.

to organize your favourite Web sites

Select the **Favorites** pull-down menu and use your mouse to organize the list. For example, you can right-click items you do not use, then select **Delete** to remove items from the **Favorites** list.

to create and send invitations
Open Outlook Express. Select <u>C</u>ompose and <u>N</u>ew Message, then select from templates on the list.

to subscribe to Web sites through channels – for free
Channels automatically deliver updated information to you from sources you select. To access this feature use the standard buttons on your toolbar. To make them appear, select <u>T</u>oolbar, then <u>S</u>tandard. On the toolbar, select **Channels**, then select the channel you wish to view from the menu. If the channel you select requires plug-ins, and if you do not have the required ones, you should allow the automatic installation of the required plug-ins.

You can record below your personal notes about Microsoft Internet Explorer or another browser.

_____

_____

_____

_____

_____

_____

using the World Wide Web productively

The Net is a wonderfully dynamic and informative place. But what good is information if you don't use it? If you don't take full advantage by setting up a Web site? If you don't keep up with the features of new versions of software? If you feel constrained by security issues?

This section will help you come to grips with these issues and more. There are tips on deciding whether you should have a Web site, producing Web documents, getting results from your Web site, preparing presentations for the Web, new features in Microsoft Internet Explorer, and Internet security.

to Web site or not to Web site

Have you ever wondered if it would be a good idea to set up your own Web site? Here are a few questions and answers that will help you understand Web sites better.

what is a Web site?

A Web site is a place on the World Wide Web with a distinct address called a Uniform Resource Locator or URL. The author's Web site URL is *http://www.brookebroadbent. mondenet.com/*

why have a Web site?

A Web site provides information to anyone who wants to learn more about you, an idea, or the products and services of an organization you are promoting through the Web.

what do I need to have a Web site?

You need space on a server with access to the Web, a little creativity, sound writing skills, and either knowledge of HTML tags or software that will do the tagging for you.

what are HTML tags?

If you understand the 'reveal codes' function of WordPerfect, you can understand HTML tags. They are codes surrounded by < and >. You can view the HTML tags of Web sites in most Web browsers. In Netscape Navigator open a Web site and select **View** and **Page Source**. These codes give the text its characteristics, such as font size, and set up links to other text and Web sites (see Figure 26.1).

what advice would you give people setting up their first Web site?

Make your site worth visiting by providing information that is pertinent, clear, and easy to access. Use bullets for emphasis. Make your site graphically interesting, but do not exaggerate the number of pictures you use or the colours that slow down the transmission of your information. Test your site using low-end hardware to ensure that people with older equipment enjoy reasonable reception.

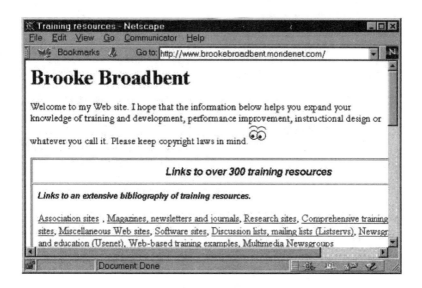

```
< HTML >
< HEAD >
< META HTP-EQUIV = 'Content-Type' CONTENT =
'text/html; charset = windows-1252' >
< META NAME = 'Generator' CONTENT = 'Microsoft
Word 97' >
< TITLE > Training resources < /TITLE >
< META NAME = 'Template' CONTENT =
'C:\PROGRAM FILES\MICROSOFT OFFICE\html.dot' >
< /HEAD >
< BODY LINK = '#0000ff' VLINK = '#800080'
BACKGROUND = 'Image6.jpg' >
```

Figure 26.1 *Example of a Web site and some of the HTML coding that makes it possible*

producing Web documents

New versions of software are designed with the Web in mind. For example, the latest versions of Microsoft® Word® and Corel® WordPerfect® have the ability to help you prepare Web-ready documents including an index, forms and graphics. (I used Word 97 to prepare the Web site pictured in Figure 26.1.) Here are a few hints on preparing online documents using Microsoft Word and Corel WordPerfect.

preparing Web documents using Microsoft Word

what is a Web document?
Web documents are information on the Internet or an intranet you can access with your browser.

how do I prepare them?
Save an existing word processing file, for example, in the HTML format under the **File** menu. Alternatively, you can get

coaching as follows. In WordPerfect select **File, Internet Publisher** and **New Web Document,** and follow the instructions (see Figure 27.1). In Microsoft Word, select **File, New** and **Web Page,** and follow the instructions (see Figure 27.2).

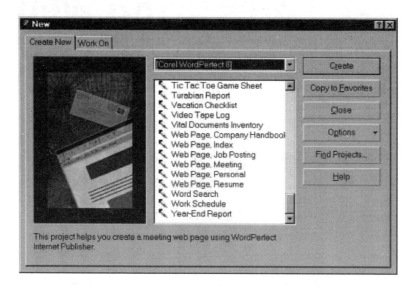

Figure 27.1 *Creating a Web document in Corel WordPerfect*

how do I put my documents on the Web?

You will have to upload your file to a server connected to the Web. Contact your ISP to see how this done in your situation. WebPost is a wizard, available on the Office97 CD ROM that takes you through the steps of posting a document to the Web.

how would I create Web documents without using these experts or wizards in Word?

If you have a good knowledge of Web pages and HTML, you can create Web documents from scratch in Word. Select **File, New** and use the menu to create your page (see Figure 27.2).

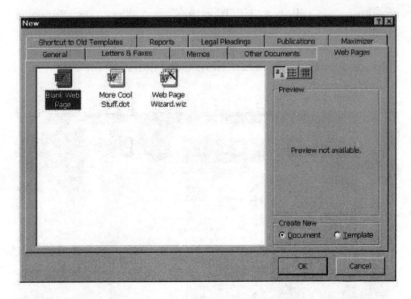

Figure 27.2 *Creating a Web document in Microsoft Word*

what can I do if I am not satisfied with the Web pages I can produce with my word processor?

Try the Web authoring tools in versions 4 and above of Netscape and Explorer. In Netscape Page Composer there is a wizard at **File, New, Page from Wizard.** There is a good shareware HTML editor called Hot Dog at *www.sausage.com* There are several Web publishing packages on the market. The Corel® WebMaster suite helps with Web page design, Web site management and database publishing, and includes over 8,000 Internet-ready images.

weaving results into your Web site

Preparing a Web page is a fair bit of work, so you will want to get a high rate of return on your investment of time and effort. How do you measure results? Here are some hints for Web page success.

how to find out how many people visit your site

A counter will help, but be certain you know what it is counting. For more information see Yahoo! Select **Computers and Internet,** then **Software,** and then search **Access counter.** If you have an ISP, check to see what they support. You may be able to cut and paste the scripts you need from their Web site.

how to find out who visits your site

You can use software to analyse who visits your site and where they are from. This way you will be able to determine whether it is worth your time to invest further in a Web site. You can also select geographical areas for future expansion of your business, based on the location of the people who visit your site.

how to ensure that people visit your Web site

Add your URL to your business card, stationery and fax cover sheet. Register your site with Web search tools such as Lycos. To do this, go to the main site of the search tools and locate a button that lets you register. You can register your Web site with several search tools by using a submittal service. Several are listed at Yahoo! Select **Computers and Internet**, then **World Wide Web**, and then select **Announcements Services**.

how to get positive comments from visitors to your site

Check your links regularly to ensure they are up-to-date. Provide useful information. Solicit feedback on a form.

how to provide up-to-date information

Separate information that needs updating so that it is easy to revise. Assign the task of updating to a specific person in your organization. Set up a schedule for updating.

how to keep people coming to your site

Provide useful information. For example, if you have written articles or other pieces that will interest potential Web site visitors, place them on your Web site.

how to learn who visits your site

Your ISP may agree to provide you with a list, or log, of visitors to your Web site. You can obtain shareware to analyse these logs at *http://www.tucows.com/* In the search area, type in 'analyse logs' and a list of software will appear.

how to promote your site every day

Place your Web site URL in your e-mail signature. If you participate in discussions on electronic mailing lists, refer people to your site for information.

spinning online presentations for the Web

Microsoft® PowerPoint® offers an easy way to make stylish Web presentations that advertise your company on the Web, provide training information to company employees or do anything else you have planned for the Internet or intranets. You can make a Web presentation by following two easy steps. First, prepare a presentation in PowerPoint. Next convert it to HTML, the Web authoring language. Here are the steps:

1. Launch Powerpoint 97.
2. Select the **AutoContent wizard** from the opening dialog box. Select **Presentation type**. Select **Personal, Personal Home Page, Finish.**
3. **AutoContent wizard** will help you prepare a template. You will need to make changes to personalize the document with your information.
4. Prepare your presentation.
5. Convert your sample presentation to an HTML document right away using **Save as HTML** in the **File** pull-down menu. Place the new document in a new folder. Use a long descriptive name for easy retrieval.

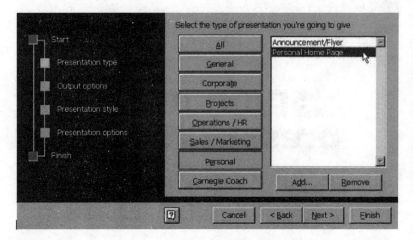

Figure 29.1 *Creating a Web presentation in PowerPoint*

creating hyperlinks in your Web page

You can create hyperlinks in a presentation so that users can jump to a specific place in your presentation, to another presentation, to a Word document, or to any spot on the Net. To create these hyperlinks do the following:

1. In PowerPoint, select **Outline** View or **Slide** View, and mark text that you want to hyperlink.
2. In the **Insert** menu, select **Hyperlink** (CTRL + K). In the **Insert Hyperlink** dialog box, add the URL or a location of a file that you wish to link to.
3. Test your Web site and links by launching your browser. Select **File**, **Open**, and browse for the HTML files generated by PowerPoint. Select the file named 'index.html' in the folder you created in step 5 of the previous table.

4. Your Internet Service Provider can advise you on how to add your developed materials to your Web site.
5. After you have uploaded files to your Web site, check out all your links using a different computer from the one on which you prepared your Web pages. This is the best test for links. If the other computer has a different screen resolution from yours and different versions of software, this will help you to conduct a thorough test.

practice makes good Web sites

Making PowerPoint presentations is a skill. Experience leads to proficiency. So roll up your sleeves and make a few. It's better to experiment now than in the heat of the action when you have only a few hours to prepare a critical presentation.

plan your work and work your plan

When cars were introduced around one hundred years ago, they were not immediately successful. Horseless carriages were expensive. People were notoriously poor drivers. It was a huge transition from coaxing the old grey mare to steering mechanical marvel. Potholes made roads difficult to navigate. It was years before motorized vehicles replaced the trusted horse. To put things in perspective, at one time there was a law requiring that a runner precede a horseless carriage along the road. It seems hard to believe now.

In the future, computer-literate generations may look back and have difficulty understanding why everyone did not embrace the Net immediately. Computers – like cars at the turn of the century – are still expensive for many people. This is especially true when you need to replace your hardware frequently in order to have the disk space, memory, processing power and multimedia features to use the latest software. Moreover, it is a big transition from a paper-based world to digital technology. Our roads, the 'information superhighways', have their share of potholes, bottlenecks and dangerous curves. Broken links, out-of-date URLs, busy signals when

dialling for a hookup to the Net, garbled e-mail attachments –
these are a few of a cybernaut's least favourite things.

my plan to drive more safely on the Web

Throughout this book, we have been considering driving tips
for the Web. You can use the space below to do some personal
planning for your future trips on the Web.

Topics for you to consider	Your notes
1. An area where you need business or personal information and the Net might help	
2. Skills and knowledge you will be working to develop	
3. Strategies you will use to develop your skills and knowledge	
4. Software you would like to investigate	
5. How you plan to investigate the above software	
6. Search engine that you will use to gather information for topic number 1	
7. Wording you will use in the search tool query	
8. Title of folder for saving information	
9. Security concerns	

managing your surfing time and costs

Thanks to its openness, the Net provides an incredible opportunity for learning and communication. But there are also dangers to be aware of. How can I keep my surfing costs down? What can I do to protect my system from viruses? How can I safely order online? What about spam? What about cookies? Stay tuned for information to help you answer these questions and others.

Some fortunate people have unlimited Internet access. Others pay for a maximum number of hours of access in a month. If they exceed their maximum, they pay a supplement. So they need to manage the amount of time they spend online. Here are some tips to keep surfing time down and manage the cost.

Download files at off-peak time, preferably early in the morning. Connections work more efficiently at this time and your file will download faster.

Learn how to use search tools effectively so that you are not wasting your time on a wild goose chase. (See pages 22–25 for hints on using search tools.)

If the delivery of graphics to your site is slowing down Netscape Navigator, turn them off by selecting **Edit, Preferences** and **Advanced**. Remove the check mark from beside **Automatically load images** by clicking on it.

Recent versions of browsers automatically place Web page files on the hard drive of your computer. You can disconnect from your service provider and still view the Web pages from your hard drive.

Exercise discipline when you are online. Stick to the original intent of your search.

Use software that keeps track of the total hours you spend online. Some ISPs offer this service to their Web sites. Software for keeping track of Net usages time is freely available on the Net. (See pages 26–27 for more information.)

If you use a modem connection and have an account with a limited number of access hours, you should go online only to transmit messages and download e-mail messages.

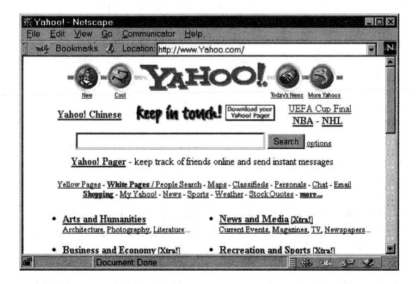

Figure 31.1   *Search tools save time*

zapping viruses

Viruses are real, but please, don't panic. My computers have been infected several times and we both survived. My first encounter with a computer virus occurred when my daughter brought a diskette home from school. It contained her project – and a virus. When Anne inserted her diskette in the floppy drive, my virus software immediately told us that Anne's diskette was infected with a virus. The software also gave us the option to remove the virus, which we did immediately, after noting other information our virus software gave us.

Recently I received the 'Concept' virus via the Internet. It installs itself in your Word macros and only lets you save documents as templates. This virus does not destroy your files or hardware, but it may distribute itself throughout your Word documents and complicate your life.

Here are a few tips on dealing with viruses.

■ *Use common sense*
Be wary. Some viruses are disguised as the ultimate utilities that claim to do impossible things. Back off. For example, when you read that a site has free software to convert your CD ROM player into a machine to duplicate CD ROMs.

▧ *Use anti-virus software*
Set up your anti-virus software to run when you turn on your computer, or boot it up. Configure your virus detection software to scan everything you download from the Net.

▧ *Learn about virus software*
Activity-monitoring programs (such as SECURE and FlutShot +) check your files for viruses as you are copying, editing, and so on. Scanners (such as FindVirus, Frisk Software's F-PROT, and McAfee's VirusScan) look for viruses in the files on your drives. Integrity checkers (ASP Integrity Toolkit, Integrity Master and VDS) check for damage or problems with your hardware. You can use search tools to find the Web sites of vendors of the software listed above.

▧ *Backup, then backup some more*
New viruses are devised daily and your version of anti-virus software may not catch newer viruses. So back up your files regularly. If a virus strikes and wipes you out, at least you will have a backup of your work.

virus alert!

From time to time my friends send me virus warnings. Some are useful and others are just plain silly. Here is a message I received recently. I was almost taken in until I remembered that viruses only come with attachments, not straight e-mail messages.

virus warning

'If you receive an e-mail with a subject of Badtimes, delete it immediately WITHOUT reading it. This is the most dangerous e-mail virus yet. It will re-write your hard drive. Not only that, but it will scramble any disks that are even close to your computer.

It will recalibrate your refrigerator's coolness setting so your ice cream melts and your milk curdles. It will demagnetize the strips on your credit cards, screw up the tracking on your VCR, and use subspace field harmonics to render any compact discs you try to play unreadable.

It will give your ex-boy/girlfriend your new phone number. It will mix antifreeze into your fish tank. It will drink all your beer and leave your dirty socks out on the coffee table when there's company coming over. It will put a dead kitten in the back pocket of your good suit and hide your car keys when you are late for work.

Badtimes will pour sugar in your petrol tank and shave off both your eyebrows. It will date your current boy/girlfriend behind your back and bill the dinner and hotel room to your Visa card. It will move your car randomly around car parks so you can't find it. It will kick your dog. It will leave libidinous messages on your boss's voice mail in your voice.

It is insidious and subtle. It is dangerous and terrifying to behold. It is also a rather interesting shade of mauve. These are just a few of the signs...'

the keys to Internet security

Christine, an ardent Netscape user, wanted to purchase a book from a vendor on the Web. She wondered whether she should make purchases via the Web. Should she type her credit card number into the Web order forms? Here are some of the facts to consider about Web purchases.

what is the source of the problem?
Information travelling between your computer and a server can be routed through many computer systems. Any one of these computer systems could capture and misuse your information.

what could happen?
Any of these computers could eavesdrop and make copies of your information. An intermediary computer could even deceive and exchange information with you by misrepresenting itself as your intended destination.

is there a complete solution?
Security technology does not protect you from dishonest or careless people with whom you might do business. The situation is similar to telling someone your credit card number

over the telephone. You have to decide whether you trust the person and the company.

what can I do?

Protect yourself by dealing with secure sites. Your software has security warnings that you can turn on to indicate if sites are secure. Unfortunately, people are not rushing to register their sites as being secure. Symbols on browsers indicate if sites are secure. For example, in Netscape Navigator, a closed lock indicates a secure site.

what is the next step?

Learn about Security in Netscape from the **Security Info** page in Netscape Communicator. To access this information, select the security icon (see figure 33.1).

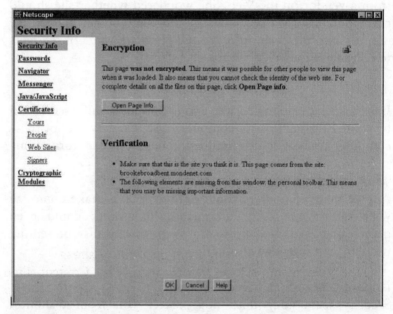

Figure 33.1 *The Security Info page in Netscape appears when you select the security icon*

feeling secure in Internet Explorer and Netscape

Paying attention to Internet security can help you to avoid viruses that can wipe out your computer, prevent unauthorized use of your credit card number, and screen out unwanted pornography. It is important that you be thorough in your security set-up. Otherwise, you will think you are secure when you are not. False security is worse than no security.

how do I change or look at my Internet Explorer security options?
On the **View** menu, select **Options**, then select the **Security** tab.

how can I decide whether to download software to my computer?
When the 'Authenticode' code certificate appears, you can decide whether to download the software.

how do I know if I have a secure connection?
Before divulging your credit card number at a Web site, look for the image of a lock on the Internet Explorer status bar at the bottom of your computer screen.

what constitutes a safe password?
At a minimum, your password should be at least six characters long, include both numbers and letters, and be in upper and lower case.

how do I protect my family from unsavoury sites?
On the **View** menu, select **Options**, then select **Content**. Find the **Ratings** area and select the **Enable** button. Set a password and select the content you want to avoid (Language, Nudity, Sex and/or Violence).

Protect yourself by dealing with secure sites. Your software has security warnings that you can turn on to indicate if sites are secure. Unfortunately, people are not rushing to register their sites as being secure. Symbols on browsers indicate if sites are secure. For example, in Netscape Navigator, a closed lock indicates a secure site.

what is the next step?

You can learn about personal *certificates* and how to obtain them in the Security info page in Netscape. (Click the Security icon on the toolbar.) Under the category Certificates, you will find links that show your certificates, certificates from other people or organizations, Web site certificates, and others.

is it safe to purchase something over the Web with a credit card?

We have seen that there is no simple answer. Thousands of people do use a credit card to make purchases over the Web. It is your money and your call.

It takes a while for services like Content Advisor in Internet Explorer to be fully operational. If you find that sites are not registered and users are excluded from everyday sites, you might want to postpone using Content Advisor until the sites, even common Microsoft ones, are registered.

canning spam

When keen Net users, sometimes called cybernauts, use the term 'spam', they are referring to unsolicited e-mail, sent to a large number of people. There term has a colourful origin in a Monty Python skit where Vikings sang the praises of spam – an ironic tribute in the minds of people who consider SPAM® Luncheon Meat to be of dubious nutritional value.

If you post messages to newsgroups and mailing lists and make your e-mail address available to spammers, chances are you will start to receive a few servings of spam daily. I receive spam on average four times a day. The last three spam messages I received promised 'to let you in on the TRUTH about doing business from your home', 'ADVERTISE FREE AND GET DRAMATICALLY MORE RESPONSES THAN ADVERTISING ON NATIONAL TELEVISION', 'TURN YOUR COMPUTER INTO A MEGA MONEY MACHINE'.

Here are a few thoughts about spam.

why do we have spam?
There are previous few rules governing the Net. Some people have taken advantage of this situation.

is spam just a nuisance or can it bring me grief?
It is mostly a nuisance but people have been burned. Folks responding to a spam offer for free pornography were tagged

for huge phone bills to Moldavia, part of the former Soviet Union.

can I trust a spammer to remove me from a list?

Some spam messages invite recipients to be removed from the list by sending a message back to the spammer. In some places this is required by law. It seems that if you send a removal message it will confirm to the spammer that your e-mail address is legitimate and you may receive more spam.

can I filter out spam?

Most e-mail programs allow you to filter out messages. For example, you could filter the e-mail addresses of specific spam artists to go directly to 'trash.'

is there anti-spam software I can use?

You will find some anti-spam tools at *http://www.tucows. com/* Simply search on 'spam'.

where can I get more information about spam?

Type **find spam** or **find junk mail** in the address bar of Internet Explorer. At the time of writing, Yahoo! has a link to an opinionated essay by Bill Gates about spam. You can find it by searching for his name on the Yahoo! site. While you are at Yahoo! you can review several sources of information about spam. Here are some of the better known sites with spam information: Death to Spam, *www.mindworkshop.com/ alchemy/nospam.html*; Spam Delenda Est (Latin for 'Spam Must Be Destroyed'), *http://www.stentorian.com/antispam/*

accepting cookies from strangers

My neighbour, Jill, recently reported that she had found several dozen cookies on her computer and deleted them. Should she have done that? What are cookies? Are they of any value?

what are cookies?
When you go to some Web sites, the Web site computer writes information (a cookie) to your hard drive. The next time you visit the same Web site, the server can retrieve the cookie and examine it.

why do we have cookies?
Cookies were devised to maintain user information and to customize Web sites. They can track users' transactions on a Web-based shopping site, or count how many times a user visits a site. Cookies can also post personal greetings, and store passwords and user names so that a subscriber won't have to re-enter them at each visit to a site.

what are the advantages?

Cookies use the Web's ability to offer customized content. They are like a salesperson or a hairdresser that gets to know a client's name, preferences and habits on the client's Web site.

If you fill in a registration form at a site it might create a cookie. When this cookie is placed on your computer, you will not be required to fill out another registration form when you return to the Web site that placed the cookie on your computer.

what are the disadvantages?

Cookies represent a potential loss of privacy. This makes some people uncomfortable. They are insidious. You do not know they are on your machine. Unless... (see next item).

what can you do about cookies?

You can block out cookies, limit or be made aware of cookie files. In Internet Explorer 4 or 5, select **View**, select **Options**, then from the **Options** dialog box, select **Advanced**. In the **Options** dialog box, find **Cookies** and select **Warn before accepting cookies.**

should I delete any cookies?

To see how many cookie files you have, search for a file folder called 'cookies' (or 'cook*'). On my computer it is under the Windows file folder. You decide if you want to delete them.

where can I learn more?

There are a large number of cookie resources on the Net. Try using the search techniques discussed earlier in the book.

You will find some anti-cookie tools at *http://www.tucows. com/*

looking ahead

personal action plan to learn more about the Net

The intent of this book is to help you learn the skills required for using the Net on your own. Here is an opportunity for you to identify the gaps in your knowledge, and develop an action plan to learn more about the Net.

Critical questions	Helpful topics in this book	My plans
What I plan to learn		
How I plan to learn		
Whom or what I plan to consult		
Other considerations		

paying attention to Bill the Gatekeeper

Microsoft has shipped more than 100 million copies of Windows since its introduction. You may not agree with everything Microsoft Chairman Bill Gates says, however his words are important. If Bill Gates says the Web is going to develop in a certain way, chances are he is already moving it in that direction. The following statements are quoted from the Microsoft Web site. Bill Gates also included most of these ideas in his speech for the launching of Internet Explorer 4.

what do you think the future holds for Web users?

People are being moved 'to think of the Web as part of their everyday lifestyle, in much the same way... they take the phone for granted, they take the car for granted, they take the TV for granted'.

what do you predict for the future?

'A decade from now, the majority of Americans will be living a Web lifestyle... they will all turn to the Web several times a day for information, for entertainment, and to communicate. ... Business cards will have an electronic mail address. Every lawyer, every doctor, every small business will be connected to the Web.'

where do we see your predictions for the future, coming true today?

At 'college campuses... all the ingredients have come together to generate the critical mass for people to take the Web as a given: There is a high-speed networkin. ... Students and staff are willing to dispense with paper forms, and to use the Web to sign up for classes, to see what their grades are.'

where are we going to get the time to live a Web lifestyle?
Part of the time comes from 'doing things more efficiently than you would have in the past – being able to get information about a major purchase, for example, or finding out how much your used car is worth'.

Web sites

In some ways, the following list of Web sites resembles a bibliography. Like a bibliography, it provides a list of sources to consult for additional information. However, it is a list of URLs (universal resource locators) or Web site addresses – not books. As a result, there are some big differences between this list and a bibliography. With books, there is consistency, stability and continuity. If you look on page 23 of a book today and a year from now, you will find the same information. Do not expect such consistency from Web sites. They are as dynamic as you can imagine and I can guarantee you that some sites listed below will change their address. Others will have new information. Some will no longer exist. Such is life on the Web. Change on the Web is often synonymous with progress, so be patient. Use the list with the proviso that it is dynamic and enjoy the richness of the Web. It is a wonderful world where you can learn, build relationships, and identify commercial opportunities.

associations

American Society for Training and Development
Founded in 1944, ASTD is one of the world's premiere professional association in the field of workplace learning and performance. ASTD's membership includes more than 65,000

individuals and organizations from every level of the field of workplace performance in more than 100 countries.
http://www.astd.org/

International Society for Performance Improvement
The International Society for Performance Improvement (ISPI) is the leading association dedicated to increasing productivity in the workplace through the application of performance and instructional technologies. Founded in 1962, its 10,000 international and chapter members are located throughout the United States, Canada and 40 other countries.
http://www.ispi.org/

International Society for Technology in Education
The International Society for Technology in Education (ISTE) promotes appropriate uses of technology to support and improve teaching and learning. Representing more than 40,000 educators, ISTE provides a curriculum for learning about technology and integrating it into the classroom, research results and project reports, and leadership for policy affecting educational technology.
http://www.iste.org/

business news

Yahoo!
http://www.yahoo.com/business/ (also *http://uk.yahoo.com/*)

training and education

Educom
'Educom is a nonprofit consortium of higher education institutions that facilitates the introduction, use, and access to and

management of information resources in teaching, learning, scholarship, and research. Educom believes that education and information technology (IT) will provide the most significant enhancements for human capability over the coming decade and that IT will have a fundamental impact upon education's ability to fulfill its mission.'

http://www.educom.edu/

The MASIE Center

The MASIE Center is an international thinktank located in Saratoga Springs, NY. The Center is dedicated to exploring the intersection of learning and technology. 'We are focused on these key areas: How do people learn to use technology? How can technology be used to help people learn? New models for providing learning across distance and time. New roles for training and learning professionals.'

http://www.masie.com/

Targeted Communications Management

Using Technology to Enhance Business Effectiveness. Includes over 130 non-commercial links.

http://www.tcm.com

Training SuperSite

Training SuperSite is 'your first stop for training resources on the Internet. Many partners have been brought onto the site to deliver the most comprehensive collection of resources available anywhere.'

http://www.trainingsupersite.com/index.htm

current events

CNN – Europe
http://www.cnn.com/WORLD/europe

education information service

AskERIC
http://ericir.syr.edu/

Microsoft information

Product information, product support, tips, and subscribe
to a newsletter
http://www.microsoft.com/

netscape information

Netscape
http:www.netscape.com/

news service

BBC Online
http://www.bbc.co.uk

shareware and freeware

c-net's Shareware.com
http://www.shareware.cnet.com/

TUCOWS
http://www.tucows.com

travel

Excite Travel
http://www.excite.com/travel/

writing

Online Writing Lab, Purdue University
http://owl.english.purdue.edu/

21st-century 'cyberspeak'

Words are the essence of communication. If you don't speak the lingo, it is impossible to communicate well. Throughout this book, I've attempted to clarify the meaning of current Net terminology. What about the future? What new cybernetic words will become common? It is impossible to be certain, but here are a few new terms that keep cropping up and may be commonplace tomorrow.

Terms	Meanings	What is in it for you
Push technology	Push technology, or Webcasting, enables Web sites to deliver their content directly to to users' desktop computers.	Notifies you automatically when your favourite Web sites have changed and lets you read those pages – even when you're not connected to the Internet.
Dynamic HTML	Web authors can control the appearance and behaviour of every element of a Web page. They can change any aspect of a page's content, such as text and graphics, without reloading.	Helps create rich, interactive Web sites. For example, when a user passes the cursor over a graphic, the Web page might expand the graphic to show greater detail.
Teledesic Network	An 'Internet-in-the-sky' with several hundred satellites orbiting close to the earth. Backed by Microsoft Chairman Bill Gates, and scheduled to begin service in 2002.	Promises affordable, high-speed telecommunications anywhere in the world. May bring incredible speed and image quality to the Internet.

glossary of terms

Account – It allows you to access the Web. If you have an Internet Service Provider (ISP), you will have an account.

ActiveX – This is a plug-in that brings multimedia (sounds, pictures, videos) to Internet Explorer, the computer program or browser that allows you to hook up to the Net.

Address – See Internet address.

Adobe Acrobat Reader – Normally a computer with the Windows operating system cannot read (use) a computer file generated by a personal computer using an operating system such as Macintosh, UNIX, Sun, or others. With Adobe Acrobat and Adobe Acrobat Reader, you can view a document on the screen of your Windows system that was created by a colleague or client using another operating system. Files read by the Adobe Acrobat Reader end in the three-letter extension pdf – meaning portable document format.

Apple QuickTime – Running under Windows as well as the Macintosh environment, QuickTime brings animation, audio, music, MIDI and video to your computer screen.

Application – Also called a computer program. A set of instructions written in computer code that enables a computer to perform specific tasks – normally with some help from the user.

Article – Name given to a message posted to a newsgroup; for example, normally asking for or giving information.

Attachment – An electronic file that you fix to an e-mail message and send with it. For example, you could send a computer file of a Microsoft Word document to a colleague, friend, relative or client.

Bandwidth – The maximum number of bits per second delivered by a network or the amount of information transmitted over a communications link. Bandwidth is important because it is a determining factor in setting the speed that information flows around the world and into your computer.

Baud – The number of signalling elements that can be transmitted per second on a circuit. Used in referring to the speed at which a modem transmits data. This is an older term being replaced by bps, bits per second. Modems are still referred to by their baud rate.

Bit – The smallest unit of measure of computer data.

Bookmark – A term used in Netscape to describe a Web site that is marked for later reference. Called a 'Favorite' in Internet Explorer. Bookmarks offer a convenient means to retrieve pages whose locations (URLs) you have saved. You store your bookmarks in a list that is saved on your hard disk.

bps – Bits per second, the measure of a modem's speed. Often expressed in kbps, kilobits.

Browser – Net software that allows a computer to access information on the Internet or an intranet. Netscape Communicator and Internet Explorer are browsers that use a graphical interactive interface (GUI) for searching, finding, viewing and managing information.

CERN – A European-wide research laboratory located near Geneva, in Switzerland. It is considered the birthplace of Web technology. Some of the important terms defined at CERN and addressed in the glossary of terms are HTML and HTTP.

Character-based applications – Preceded Windows and the use of icons, pull-down menus and graphics. Users of character-based software see only text and numbers on the monitor screen. DOS is an example.

Chat – Chat is an Internet communication service. If you subscribe to AOL and other value-added ISPs, they have their own chat groups and software. Internet Relay Chat (IRC) and ICQ are software that sets up chat services on the Net.

Client – A computer that uses the services of another computer, called a server. When you are using the Internet to download information to your computer, your machine is a client.

Cookie – When you go to a Web site, the Web site computer writes a bit of information, called a cookie, to your hard drive. The next time you visit the same Web site, the server can retrieve the cookie and examine it. Cookies are passive – they do not grab data off your hard drive. The cookie program is a string of programming code that resides in the header of an HTTP file.

Cyberspace – The realm of computer-aided communication. Originally used in *Neuromancer*, William Gibson's novel of direct brain–computer networking.

DNS (Domain Name Server) – A computer on the Internet. It does the work of translating between an Internet domain name such as abc.com and an Internet numerical address such as 123.456.78.9.

Domain or domain name – Part of a computer's official name (for example, abc.com). Your ISP can tell you more about obtaining a domain name. You can register your domain name at *http://www.internic.net/* – for a fee.

Download – To transfer programs or data from a computer to a connected device, usually from a server to your personal computer.

Dynamic HTML – An upgrade of plain vanilla HTML that was good in its time. Tagging documents with dynamic HTML, Web authors can control the appearance and behaviour of every element of a Web page. They can change any aspect of a page's content, such as text and graphics, without reloading.

E-mail – Short form for electronic mail, as opposed to regular mail, sometimes called 'snail mail', the realm of the post office.

Eudora – A popular e-mail program for Windows and Mac computers.

FAQ (Frequently Asked Questions) – A collection of questions that are commonly asked in a newsgroup or mailing list – including answers. A good place to start when you join a newsgroup or mailing list.

Flame – A rude or inflammatory Internet message. Most often occurs when you write someone complaining about something they have written to a mailing list or newsgroup. Often leads to more flaming and generally unproductive use of everyone's time and energy.

Folder – An area where you store similar material so you find it later. You should create these in Windows to store and organize the messages you receive, the Web site information you capture, and the software you download from the Net.

FTP (File Transfer Protocol) – A way of transferring data from one computer to another over the Net.

GIF (Graphics Interchange Format) – A standard format for image files on the WWW. The GIF file format is popular because it uses a compression method to make files smaller. As a result, GIF files occupy less space on your hard drive.

Gigabyte – 1,000,000,000 bytes of data. This seems to be a huge amount of data but present software takes a good bite out of a one-gigabyte hard drive.

Handle – Used in chat instead of your real name. Part of the chat masquerade party associated with recreational chat.

Home page – The first area you see on your monitor when you access a Web site.

HTML (Hyper Text Markup Language) – A 'tag' language used to format Web pages. To see HTML coding, load a Web page in Netscape Navigator 4, select <u>V</u>iew, Page Source.

HTTP (Hyper Text Transfer Protocol) – the method used to transfer documents from the host computer or server to browsers and individual users. Commonly seen as the first letters of most URLs, or Internet addresses, for example *http://www.bbc.co.uk/*

Hyperlink – Connections between one piece of information and another. In browsers, hyperlinked text is underlined.

Hypertext – Allows the user to select text and immediately display related information. You click on a hypertext link and your browser sends you to the place on the Web or a file that is associated with the address you click on.

Internet – The interconnection of thousands of computer networks worldwide. The Internet has capacity for an estimated 250 million Internet users. Data from *http://wwweuromktg.com/globstats/*

Internet address – A unique combination of letters, most of which start with HTTP.

Internet Explorer – See Microsoft Internet Explorer.

Intranet – Like an Internet at the level of an organization, most often a business. Using popular Internet software, an intranet allows people to exchange data within an organization, as they do on the Internet, with the world.

ISDN (Integrated Services Digital Network) – A digital telephone system, faster than normal telephone service, operating at a speed of up to 128 kilobits per second.

Java – A computer language that can run on any modern computer and is therefore ideal for the Internet.

JPEG (Joint Photographic Experts Group) – A popular method used to compress the size of photographic images. Many Web browsers accept JPEG images as a standard format for viewing graphics on Web pages.

Lurk – To read messages in a mailing list, newsgroup or chat group without posting messages. It is a good idea to be a lurker when you first join a group.

Mailing List – An e-mail service that 'remails' all incoming mail received by the list. Each message is sent to people who subscribe to the list, unless they arrange otherwise.

Microsoft Internet Explorer – Like Netscape, Microsoft has bundled their Internet applications in a suite. Internet Explorer consists of FrontPage Express, Microsoft Chat, NetMeeting, Outlook Express, and some other bit players. These applications can be used with the Internet or your company intranet.
FrontPage Express: This is a low-end Web-page editor. You can work in a WYSIWYG ('what you see is what you get') view. And in this way you can see how your formatting and layout will actually appear on the your Web site.
Microsoft Chat: This is an Internet chat program with the option of taking a comic strip character as your persona.
Microsoft NetMeeting: Conferencing software providing a framework for talking, meeting, working, and sharing information over the Internet and intranets.
Microsoft Outlook Express: E-mail and newsgroup software.

Mnemonic – A memory aid normally created from the first letter of a series of words.

Modem (MODulator-DEModulator) – Computer hardware that enables digital data (computer information) to be transmitted over analog transmission facilities like telephone lines.

Moderator – An important person for a moderated mailing list. The moderator or a group of moderators review the messages posted to a mailing list or some newsgroups and decide whether they can be released to the public.

Multimedia – The combining of audio, video and data. Internet browsers have multimedia capability due to the addition of plug-ins.

Net – Short form for Internet. In this book, Net also includes intranets.

Netiquette – Rules for how to behave on the Internet, especially in mailing lists, e-mail and newsgroups.

Netscape Communicator – Like Microsoft, Netscape has created a suite of Internet applications. They consist of Composer, Collabra, Conference Messenger, Navigator, and Netcaster, plus other programs that are available in the professional version of Netscape Communicator. All of these applications can be used with the Internet or intranets.

Netscape Composer: This is a low-end package for producing online documents for the Internet or intranets. The WYSIWYG ('what you see is what you get') editing helps you to create online documents and publish them to local file systems and remove servers with ease.

Netscape Collabra: Software for newsgroups. It can also help cut down on mass e-mail by disseminating company information and announcements.

Netscape Conference: It supports audio/visual conferencing and a variety of other approaches to communicating on the Net using whiteboards, chat and file transfer.

Netscape Messenger: This is Netscape's e-mail software. Among other features, the Netscape 4 version allows you to encrypt and decrypt your messages for privacy, use filters to automatically organize your incoming messages into folders, and quickly add and look up e-mail addresses.

Netscape Navigator: Netscape's browser. Can be used with the Internet or intranets to access the wealth of information in cyberspace.

Netscape Netcaster: Enables you to subscribe to and schedule automatic delivery of the information you want, from the best channels on the Web, instead of manually downloading and searching for information.

Newbie – A newcomer to the Net.

Newsgroup – A topical area in Usenet newsgroups.

Newsreader – Software that allows you to read and respond to messages in newsgroups.

Online – A comprehensive term embracing the Web, Internet and intranets.

Page – A way of collecting and conveying information on the Net. Pages may be of any length and contain a variety of elements, including text, graphics, sound and video.

PCMCIA – Compact computer accessories, mostly associated with laptop computers. A PCMCIA modem resembles a thick credit card.

Pegasus Mail – A free e-mail program with many advanced features.

Plug-in – A computer program that you add to your Internet browser to handle additional functions such as audio and video.

Protocol – Rules governing how computers talk to each other. The 'p' in HTTP, TCP/IP and other important Net conventions.

Pull-down menu – A menu appearing at the top of the screen in Windows applications. When selected, another menu drops down.

Push technology – Push technology, or Webcasting, enables Web sites to deliver their content directly to users' desktop computers.

RealAudio – With this plug-in installed in your browser, you can listen to live and on-demand audio over the Internet using your standard modem.

RealPlayer – RealPlayer is a real-time audio and video delivery system for the Internet. It is distributed with Microsoft Internet Explorer. Using RealPlayer, you can listen and view thousands of hours of live and pre-recorded clips, including sporting events, live radio stations, news, music, and lectures.

Search tool – A free service on the Net. Search tools are like master librarians that index and find links on the Internet to the information you request. When you type in a phrase or keyword, the search tool scans the pages in its index for matches.

Server – A computer that provides services to another computer – called a client.

Service provider (ISP) – A commercial company selling Internet access. Also called an Internet Service Provider or ISP.

Shareware – Computer programs that you can download from the Net. You are free to use them for a period of time – often 30 days. If you keep them longer, you are expected to pay the shareware provider.

Shockwave – Sometimes called Macromedia Shockwave. This is the most popular plug-in for viewing multimedia.

Smiley – A combination of keyboard characters that portray emotions like :-) for a smile or :-(for a frown. Also called an emoticon.

Snail mail – Traditional mail, more personalized than e-mail but slower to arrive at its destination (though postal services are changing that by introducing new ways of transmitting messages).

Spam – The verb and noun refer to sending a commercial e-mail message to a large number of people. Also used to cover a multitude of other disruptive, nasty things that happen via e-mail from time-to-time.

Spiders – Search tools send out small programs that we once called robots but now refer to as spiders, crawlers or 'indexers' – to review and catalog Web sits and copy text they find into a database.

Surfing – Looking for interesting things on the World Wide Web using search engines and hyperlinks.

Teledesic Network – An Internet-in-the-sky, with several hundred satellites orbiting close to the earth that generate fast Net communication. Backed by Microsoft Chairman Bill Gates and scheduled to begin service in 2002.

URL (Uniform Resource Locator) – A Web site address with the name of the server where the site's files are stored, the file's directory path, and its file name. For example *http://www.fka.com/*

Usenet (USE NETwork) – Internet-based discussion groups on just about any subject you can imagine.

Web page – Same thing as a Web site.

Web site – A location where Web information is collected and made available, normally to anyone with access to the Internet.

WinZip – WinZip is a compression utility that lets Windows users make their files smaller for faster transfer over the Internet. This utility also decompresses files that were originally compressed using PKZIP or TAR formats.

World Wide Web (WWW) – The World Wide Web, or Web, provides a way of linking computers on the Internet through HTML tags and using hyperlinks that allows you to click on a link and advance to another location on the Web.